Joan Nordquist

Audiovisuals for Women

McFarland
& Company, Inc., Publishers
Jefferson, N.C., 1980

Library of Congress Cataloging in Publication Data

Nordquist, Joan.
 Audiovisuals for women.

 Includes index.
 1. Women—Bibliography. 2. Women—Discography. 3. Women—Film catalogs. 4. Feminism—Bibliography. 5. Feminism—Discography. 6. Feminism—Film catalogs. I. Title.
 Z7961.N67 [HQ1206] 016.3054'2 80-14691
 ISBN 0-89950-011-0
 ISBN 0-89950-012-9 (pbk)

Copyright © 1980 by Joan Nordquist
Manufactured in the United States of America

TABLE OF CONTENTS

INTRODUCTION

    The Need for This Bibliography   v
    Scope and Limitations   vii
    Arrangement   vii

THE BIBLIOGRAPHY

    16mm Films   1
    Videotapes   32
    Filmstrips   57
    Slides   66
    Recordings/Spoken Word   74
    Recordings/Music   104
    Contemporary Filmmakers' Works   119

DIRECTORY OF DISTRIBUTORS   125

ADDITIONAL RESOURCES   134

SUBJECT INDEX   137

INTRODUCTION

The 19th- and the 20th-century feminist movements both appeared at times of unusual support for social reform. Underlying the emergence of each feminist movement has been a reformist ideology which provided a rationale for various reform movements. The 19th-century feminists believed that women's position could be reformed within the existing societal context; they believed in the 19th-century reform ethic that stated that people could, by their own efforts, make their lives personally rewarding. The reformers did not think that changes in society's institutions were necessary.

A hundred years later, a new set of feminist ideas grew out of the radical ideologies of the 1960's. One of the main ideas was that socialization, not biological factors, accounted for minority members' differences in ability, temperament and achievement. The feminist movement saw female socialization as a debilitating experience of fundamental importance. Another significant aspect of the ideology of the 1960's was the recognition that individuals were oppressed not only by other individuals and groups but also by the institutions of society. As a result, reform depended upon the structural change of society. This idea has led the feminist movement to question the organization of institutions such as the family and the traditional division of labor between the sexes.

Many feminists have concentrated on the problem of female socialization and the enhancement of the self image of women. As a result, a proliferation of information for, about and by women has appeared. Books, magazines, newsletters, films and recordings are being produced in vast amounts and at incredible speed. The dissemination of this information about women, their past, present, and future condition must be made if the information is to lead to the desired action necessary for social change.

The Need for This Bibliography

Many bibliographies on women include some nonprint material. However (as of mid-1979) these works are no longer current; the most recent surveyed prior to compiling the present book was published in 1975. Since that date much material has been produced. Also, the existing works concentrate on one type of non-book media, usually the 16mm film. The existing bibliographies on women which are concerned with audiovisual materials or which include audiovisual materials are listed below.

Association of American Colleges. Women and Film: A Resource Handbook. Washington, D.C., 1974.

Barnett, Joan, and Ann Pettingill. Women: A Bibliography of Books and Other Materials. Los Angeles: John F. Kennedy Memorial Library, California State University, 1975.

Betencourt, Jeanne. Women in Focus. Dayton, Ohio: Pflaum, Standard, 1974.

Dawson, Bonnie. Women's Film in Print: An Annotated Guide to Over 750 Films. San Francisco: Booklegger Press, 1975.

Edwards, Richard, and Bruce Gronbeck. A Partial List of Educational, Instructional and Documentary Films Treating Women's Roles, Problems and Communication Strategies. Washington, D.C.: ERIC, 1975.

Emmens, Carol. Famous People on Film. Metuchen, N.J.: Scarecrow Press, 1977.

Kowalski, Rosemary. Women and Film: A Bibliography. Metuchen, N.J.: Scarecrow Press, 1976.

Women's History Research Center. Directory of Films by and about Women. Berkeley, Calif., 1972.

Three works attempt to provide access to all forms of nonprint materials on women, particularly those works produced by women's groups and organizations. These works are:

Harrison, Cynthia. Women's Movement Media: A Sourcebook. New York: Bowker, 1975.

Media Report to Women Directory, 19--. Washington, D.C.: Women's Institute for Freedom of the Press, annual.

Wheeler, Helen. Womanhood Media, 1969; Supplement, 1975. Metuchen, N.J.: Scarecrow Press.

The Wheeler bibliography does have a selective list of nonprint media; however, the emphasis is on the 16mm film and many useful audio and video recordings are not included in the work. The Harrison book does not attempt to provide a bibliography of audiovisual materials. It gives the names and addresses of otherwise difficult-to-find nonbook media producers and distributors. The Media Report to Women Directory contains the most comprehensive and current listing of media sources (distributors, filmmakers, women's media collectives), but it also does not provide a bibliography of materials other than books. Therefore, a current, inexpensive and comprehensive nonprint media bibliography on women is needed.

Introduction

Scope and Limitations

The present work supplements the existing audiovisual bibliographies by providing access to current materials that as a class were not in the earlier works and by providing access to audiovisual materials produced since the publication of those works. The present work provides a current, annotated bibliography of audiovisual materials (motion pictures, filmstrips, audio and video recordings, and slides) for, about, and by women produced in the English language in the United States and Canada. Materials designed primarily for educational use in the elementary classroom will not be included.

The media producers and distributors listed in the works of Harrison, Wheeler, and the Media Report to Women Directory were contacted and many of the audiovisual materials listed in this bibliography were selected from their current catalogs of productions. These sources represent the main body of work produced and distributed by women in the United States and Canada. Material was also located by consulting the periodical literature produced by women's groups and organizations. And, of course, standard audiovisual selection tools were used to locate relevant material.

Arrangement

The materials are arranged by physical medium. The divisions of the material are:

16mm Films
Videotapes
Filmstrips
Slides

Recordings/Spoken Word
Recordings/Music
Contemporary Filmmakers' Works

The 16mm films are divided into two categories. The first category, "16mm Films," is for films for and about women. The other category, "Contemporary Filmmakers' Works," contains current films made by contemporary women filmmakers which are not necessarily on the subject of women. For a complete, up-to-date list of contemporary women filmmakers the Media Report to Women Directory should be consulted.

The recordings are also divided into two categories. The first, "Recordings/Spoken Word," contains all current spoken-word recordings relevant for women. The other category, "Recordings/Music," is a selection of current recordings of music produced and distributed by independent, women-operated and women-oriented record producers and distributors. For complete list of recordings, the bibliography My Sisters' Song: Women's Records by Woman's Soul Publishing, Inc., should be consulted (see Additional Resources at the end of the book.)

The notations on each item will include the title, the producer and/or distributor, the release date, and a technical description.

Evaluative comments from reviews have been provided when available. Also, sources for reviews are noted. The standard audiovisual review indexes, <u>Media Review Digest</u> and <u>International Index to Multi-Media Information</u>, were consulted. However, because many of the nonprint materials included in the bibliography were produced so recently, the review indexes did not provide much information. Therefore, the most current issues of audiovisual review sources such as <u>Booklist</u>, <u>Landers Film Reviews</u>, <u>Previews</u>, <u>Media and Methods</u>, <u>Sightlines</u>, <u>Audiovisual Instruction</u>, <u>Film News</u>, <u>Media Mix</u>, and <u>Visual Education</u> were examined for recent review literature.

A subject index has been prepared, with citations under each subject broken down by media, except the two sections entitled "Contemporary Filmmakers' Works" and "Recordings/Music." These two sections are arranged by the personal name of the filmmaker or the musical group or artist. References in the subject index are to entry numbers.

The Bibliography

16mm FILMS

1 ACCOMPLISHED WOMEN, by Charles Braverman, 1975. 26 min. color. Films Incorporated.
   Features six women who discuss a wide range of topics, all of which point to a new attitude and a new image that women have of themselves.
   Reviews: Wilson Library Bulletin, March 1975, p 525 ("lively and entertaining film about six women ... will spur women to seek high achievement"--Myra Nadler). Media and Methods, October 1975, p73. Media Mix, May 1975, p3. Previews, May 1975, p27.

2 ACT OF CONTRITION, by Diane Graham, n.d. 4 min. b/w. Women's Film Coop.
   The film provides an introduction to discussion about sexuality and women's relationship to the church.

3 AIN'T NOBODY'S BUSINESS, by Sally Barrett-Page and Ellen Grant, 1977. 52 min. color. Tomatoe Productions Incorporated.
   Documentary on female prostitution featuring scenes from six different prostitutes, a male member of the vice squad, and Margo St. James, as well as footage from the First World Meeting of Prostitutes held in Washington, D.C., in June 1976.

4 ALBUM, by Linda Heller, 1976. 5 min. color. Serious Business Company.
   Growing up female in the nuclear family and surviving with a sense of humor intact is the story of this brightly-colored family album of pop-deco drawings.

5 ALL OF US STRONGER, by Kartemquin/Hay Market, 1976. 9 min. color. Serious Business Company.
   Women learning karate, tell their self-defense experiences and how they are experiencing their own power.

6 AM I WIFE, MOTHER OR ME?, by Tomorrow Entertainment, 1975. 31 min. color. Learning Corporation of America.
   Depicts a woman's need to challenge her role as wife and mother and seek fulfillment for herself as an individual. Explores some of the difficulties she encounters and her own feelings of ambiguity.

7 THE AMERICAN PARADE -- WE THE WOMEN, by CBS News, 1974. 30 min. color. BFA Educational Media.
Examines the role of woman and the women's movement throughout history. Shows the efforts of women such as Lucretia Mott, Susan B. Anthony, Elizabeth Cady Stanton and Carrie Chapman Catt who worked for women's rights during the 19th century, and discusses the characteristics of the women's movement of the 1970's.

8 THE AMERICAN WOMAN: PORTRAITS OF COURAGE, by Concepts Unlimited Productions, 1976. 53 min. color. McGraw-Hill Films.
A series of portraits of the women who played a decisive role in the shaping of American history. The film uses rare archival illustrations, early film footage, photographs and interviews to spotlight important moments in the lives of American women.

9 ANAIS OBSERVED, by Robert Snyder, 1973. 67 min. color. Master and Masterworks Productions.
The film explores the writings and the life of Anais Nin.
Reviews: Film News, March/April 1976, p17. EFLA Evaluations, 1975, p8897.

10 AND THEY LIVED HAPPILY EVER AFTER, by Kathleen Shannon, 1976. 13 min. color. National Film Board of Canada.
A series of interviews with teenage women reveals that marriage still seems to be the ultimate realization of their ideals and selfhood. The film, by contrasting their expectations with their reality, makes a statement about cultural manipulation of women.
Review: Booklist, November 1, 1976, p350-351 ("will cause viewers to evaluate their expectations...[and] may also bolster the spirits of women who may be wondering 'What's wrong with me?' since their lives don't measure up to their fantasies").

11 ANIMATED WOMEN, by Barbara Bottner and others, n.d. 15 min. color. Texture Films, Inc.
A five-part film composed of the following animated sequences: Later That Night by Barbara Bottner, Made for Each Other by Barbara Bottner, Brews and Potions by Deborah Healy, The Ballad of Lucy Jordan by Ian Moo Young, A La Votre by Monique Renault. Women's aspirations, relationships, and power are explored.

12 ANYTHING THEY WANT TO BE, by Far West Laboratory for Educational Research and Development, 1974. 7 min. color. University of California Extension Media Center.

Explores sex role stereotypes in intellectual and career-oriented activities. Uses examples to show how girls and women are discouraged from excelling in academic and vocational pursuits and task-solving.

13 AUTOBIOGRAPHY OF A WOMAN, by Barbara Dills, Alev Little, Jean Weinberg, n.d. 20 min. color. Women's Film Coop.
A film which makes visual all the repressive forces that have kept women, especially middle-class women, in their place and at the same time given them a sense of direction.

14 BARBARA, by Diane Graham, n.d. 13 min. b/w. Women's Film Coop.
A look at the despair and repressed violence of a woman in an unhappy marriage.

15 BATTERED WIVES -- A LEGACY OF VIOLENCE, by P. Stern, 1978. 29 min. color. Women's Eye Multi Media Productions.
This film explores the historical, social, psychological, and legal implications of the problem of wife abuse. Presents viewpoints of a therapist, shelter director, the police, and scholars in the humanities. Three victims of wife abuse discuss patterns of violence.

16 BATTERED WOMEN -- VIOLENCE BEHIND CLOSED DOORS, by Michelle Gebhardt Film Company, n.d. 30 min. Michelle Gebhardt Films.
Explores attitudes of battered women and their abusers. Discusses the effects of violence on children and the use of shelters.

17 BE SOMEBODY, by Elena Erenberg, n.d. 2 min. color. Creative Film Society.
A UCLA Animation Workshop film that shows the obsession for constant change in women's fashions and women's anatomy to keep pace with current fashion.

18 BEING A PRISONER, by Kinok Film Production Company, 1975. 28 min. color. Kinok Film Production Company.
Takes a look at the lives of women in a New Jersey prison. Includes sequences with narration in Spanish with English subtitles.

19 BERNICE BOBS HER HAIR, by Joan Micklin Silver, n.d. (From a story by F. Scott Fitzgerald). 47 min. color (also available in videocassette). Perspective Films.
The film is based on the story Bernice Bobs Her Hair by F. Scott Fitzgerald. Bernice is of the pre-flapper

generation, but her struggles in learning to "fit in" are as modern as today.

20 BEST OF THE NEW YORK WOMEN'S FILM FESTIVAL, by New Line Cinema, n.d. 103 min. color. New Line Cinema.

A group of short films made entirely by women. Films are (1) Crocus by Susan Pitt Kraning, (2) Opening/Closing by Kathleen Laughlan, (3) Dirty Books by Linda Feferman, (4) Commuters by Claudia Weil, (5) Cover Girl: New Face in Focus by Frances McLaughlin Gill, (6) Cycles by Linda Jassim, (7) Gibbous Moon by Nancy Ellen Dowd, (8) Holding by Constance Beeson.

21 BILL OF RIGHTS IN ACTION: WOMEN'S RIGHTS., by BFA Educational Media, 1974. 22 min. color. BFA Educational Media.

A black high school student makes her school swimming team, but a state regulation bans girls from athletic competition. Her female attorney takes the case.

22 BIRTH CONTROL: THE CHOICES, by Churchill Films, 1976. 25 min. color. Churchill Films.

Presents the uses, limitations and side effects of the usual methods of birth control, as well as tubal ligation, vasectomy, and abortion.

23 BREAKING OUT OF THE DOLL'S HOUSE, by Learning Corporation of America, 1975. 32 min. color. Learning Corporation of America.

Edited from the 1974 motion picture, A Doll's House, an adaptation of Ibsen's play about a woman who leaves her husband and children in order to realize her own potential as a human being.

24 BUENOS DÍAS, COMPAÑEROS: WOMEN IN CUBA, by Vivienne Leebosh, 1975. 57 min. color. Phoenix Films.

Examines the lives of four women in Cuba and how the revolution has affected the status of women. The four women have lives of entirely different circumstances: Haydee, a construction forelady; Gladys, a housewife; Angelita, a farm worker; and Sara, one of Cuba's most popular singers today.

25 CAMPAIGN by Churchill Films, 1975. 20 min. color. Churchill Films.

A young woman running for state senator wages a rousing campaign with the help of volunteers.

Reviews: Ms., October 1976, p112 ("A good study of the nitty-gritty of American politics and the attitude of the media toward women candidates"--Carol Emmens). Media and Methods, December 1975, p24.

26 CAT: A WOMAN WHO FOUGHT BACK, by Champion Films, n.d. 27 min. color. Women Make Movies, Inc.

Cathy "Cat" Davis is a 24-year-old boxer. The film shows her struggle to strike down laws that have prevented women from boxing professionally and her encounters with the New York State Athletic Commission, Joe Frazier and Muhammad Ali.

27 CATHERINE, by Amelia Anderson, 1974. 22 min. b/w. Creative Film Society.

The film is a psychological drama comparing the diversely different life styles of two sisters. Eventually, both women are forced to examine values, and make choices in order to move on in life.

28 CHANGING IMAGES: CONFRONTING CAREER STEREOTYPES, by Far West Laboratory for Educational Research and Development, 1975. 16 min. b/w. University of California Extension Media Center.

The film observes a class of 4th and 5th graders change their traditional sex-role career stereotypes over a five-week period.

Review: Booklist, May 15, 1976, p1348 ("Concisely edited into a provocative statement").

29 THE CHICAGO MATERNITY CENTER STORY, by Kartemquin/Haymarket Films, 1977. 60 min. b/w. Kartemquin/Haymarket Films.

Part I., Healthcare Worth Fighting For, is about the proposed closing of the Chicago Maternity Center. A group of mothers tell why the low-cost preventive center is worth fighting for. Part 2. The Struggle for Control, provides an historical analysis of why modern medicine rejects this center's approach in favor of high-cost, hospital-based care. The black, Latin, and white mothers confront the Board of Directors of the Center and, though supported by the community, the women fail to keep the Center open.

30 CHINAMOON, by Barbara Linkevitch, 1975. 15 min. color. Serious Business Company.

Experimental and impressionistic in technique, the movie centers around the formally ritualized world of a room inhabited by four prostitutes. They are depicted with tenderness and sensitivity; not as sex objects, but tragically, as tired, sexually depleted women.

31 CHISHOLM: PURSUING THE DREAM, by Bob Denby, 1975. 42 min. color. New Line Cinema.

Documentary about Congresswoman Shirley Chisholm and her campaign for the 1972 presidential nomination.

Women's Nonprint Media   6

Reviews: Wilson Library Bulletin, March 1975, p525 ("presents a literate person seriously campaigning against overwhelming odds to become the first black and woman President of the United States"--Myra Nadler). Ms., October 1976, p112. Booklist, January 1, 1975, p448. Film Library Quarterly Vol. 8, #1, 1975, p52. Film News, December 1974, p64. Media and Methods December 1975, p64.

32 A CIRCLE IN THE FIRE, by Victor Nunez, n.d. 49 min. color. Perspective Films.
An excellent introduction to the world of Flannery O'Connor. The film is based on her short story A Circle in the Fire.

33 CIRCLES II, by Doris Chase, n.d. 8 min. color (also available on videocassette). Perspective Films.
This Doris Chase film demonstrates sculptures made specifically for dancers. The dance and sculpture are both kinetic within their own forms, then they form new dynamics between the forms and people moving.

34 CLORAE AND ALBIE, by Joyce Chopra, 1975. 36 min. color. National Institute of Education Development Center.
Two young black women try to put their lives back together. One woman, divorced with children, goes back to high school; the other decides to go to college.
Reviews: Media and Methods, February 1977, p10 ("This technically excellent film offers many intimate glimpses into the lives of these two women.")

35 COLLAGE: MINNESOTA WOMEN IN THE ARTS, by Twin Cities Women's Film Collective, n.d. 28 min. color. Femme Films, Inc.
Traces the history of women artists in Minnesota linking the creative Indian and European foremothers to the women artists of today.

36 A COMEDY IN SIX UNNATURAL ACTS, by Jan Oxenberg, 1975. 25 min. b/w. Iris Films.
A satire of some of the stereotyped images of lesbians, filmed in various styles which are spoofs on different genres of Hollywood films.

37 COMING TO KNOW, by Marie Ashton, 1976. 9 min. b/w. Serious Business Company.
Two young women discuss how they discovered their sexual interest in women. In a straightforward, candid manner they relate early experiences through which they became aware of being gay.

38 COURAGE TO SUCCEED, by Saxton Communications

Group, Ltd., n.d. 28 min. color. Texture Films. Inc.

Diana Nyad is the world's first-ranked woman marathon swimmer. The film shows several of her swimming events and explores her thoughts on being an athlete.

39 CRYSTAL LEE JORDAN, by Joan Fiore, 1976. 16 min. color. Indiana University Audiovisual Center.

The film follows Crystal Lee Jordan, a wife, mother and blue-collar worker, in her attempt to unionize textile mill workers in Roanoke Rapids, North Carolina.

Review: Ms., Ocotober 1976, p111.

40 DADDY DON'T BE SILLY--A CASE FOR EQUAL RIGHTS, by NetDivision, Educational Broadcasting Corporation, 1975. 27 min. color. Indiana University Audiovisual Center.

History of the struggle for women's rights is portrayed. Interviews with anti-ERA people state their case. The case for ERA is expressed by showing three examples of discrimination.

Reviews: Previews, October 1976, p29 ("will be useful in any area in which consciousness-raising is desired"--Eleanor Hoehn). Booklist, November 15, 1975, p463. Media and Methods, October 1975, p74.

41 A DAY OF PLANE HUNTING, by Newsreel, n.d. 20 min. b/w. Newsreel.

Footage of the crucial role that Vietnamese women played in the war. Shows the total participation of women in production, education, and in combat. New methods of child care and in carrying out the other activities of daily life are illustrated. Vietnamese language soundtrack with English subtitles.

42 DEAL ME IN, by Patricial Colbert, n.d. 30 min. color. University of South Florida.

Portrays nine Florida women who have broken out of the low-pay, low-status job ghetto to find rewarding careers in the skilled trades, engineering, agriculture and management.

43 DEBORAH SAMPSON: A WOMAN IN REVOLUTION, by Greenhouse Films, 1975. 15 min. color. BFA Educational Media.

A biography of Deborah Sampson who, under an assumed name and identity, served in the Revolutionary Army. She took an active part in the Battles of Tarrytown and Yorktown.

Review: Previews, November 1976, p21. ("for those of us who are drowning in a sea of mediocre materials related to the Bicentennial or the Women's Movement, here is a film which provides welcome relief...").

Women's Nonprint Media   8

44 A DETERMINING FORCE, by the National Council of Churches, n.d. 60 min. color. National Council of Churches.

The film describes the place of women in the church during the Middle Ages. The documentary shows Mont St. Michel, Chartres and Notre Dame cathedrals as it sets the scene of the place of women in the church at this time. Four women are described: Catherine of Siena, Katherin Zell, wife of a leading reformer, Elizabeth I of England, and Margaret Fell Fox, the Quaker.

45 DIARY OF MISS ANNIE ANDERSON, by Rich and Spratling Production Company, 1976. 30 min. color. Soho Cinema.

At 94, Annie Anderson is one of America's last pioneers. For many years she has been writing a personal history which has been made into a film to dramatize the adventures and struggles of American women.

46 A DISCUSSION OF SHIRLEY JACKSON'S THE LOTTERY, by Encyclopaedia Britannica Educational Corp., 1969. 10 min. b/w. Encyclopaedia Britannica Educational Corp.

Presents a commentary on the famous short story, written and presented by Dr. James Durbin, associate professor of English at the University of Southern California.

47 THE DISPLACED PERSON, by Horton Foote and Glenn Jordan. n.d. 57 min. color (also available on videocassette). Perspective Films.

The Displaced Person is a short story by Flannery O'Connor.

48 DO I REALLY WANT A CHILD?, by Hanley Thompson Associates, Inc. 28 min. color. Learning Corporation of America.

A drama which examines the dilemma of a happily-married 40-year-old career woman who has to decide whether she really wants to start a family.

Reviews: Previews, September 1976, p22 ("Because the concern centers so much on the fact that the wife is over forty and a very successful career woman, young marrieds and the young adults will relate very little to the film. As a film it is an excellent production with good color, well directed and well written"--Janet Pollacheck). Mass Media, November 10, 1975, p2. Media and Methods, October 1975, p73. Landers Film Reviews, November/December 1976, p66.

49 DOES ANYBODY NEED ME ANYMORE?, by Learning Corporation of America, 1975. 29 min. color. Learning Corporation of America.

A dramatization showing the reevaluation of a group of women involved in consciousness-raising. Social roles are redefined and the reactions and changes of the husbands and wives are explored.

Reviews: <u>Previews</u>, January 1977, p13 ("The problem is presented, and while some couples are shown failing for various reasons, featured is an effective solution through self-realization, growth and adaptability"--Lenore Bayus). <u>Mass Media</u>, November 10, 1975, p2. <u>Media and Methods</u>, October 1975, p73. <u>Landers Film Reviews</u>, November/December 1976, p66.

50 DOUBLE DAY, by the International Women's Film Project, 1975. 56 min. color. Tricontinental Film Center.

A social documentary about women workers in Latin America. The women are interviewed in Spanish and speak of the social and political conditions in their countries today. The narration is in English.

Review: <u>Previews</u>, November 1976, p21 (filmed with the greatest sensitivity to caste, class, tradition, context and feminism ... [this] film presents a compassionate statement about the increased political consciousness among women workers"--Renee Feinberg).

51 DOUBLE VISION: WOMEN IN EDUCATION IN MINNESOTA. Twin Cities Women's Film Collective, n.d. 30 min. color. Femme Films, Inc.

The film includes historical photos, live interviews, classroom scenes, and reenactments of notable women in past and present education issues in Minnesota.

52 ELIZA, by WNET-TV, 1977. 28 min. color (videocassette also). Films Incorporated.

The story of Eliza Lucas Pinckney, who managed a plantation in 18th-century South Carolina. Seeking new crops, she experimented with the growing of indigo and by 1747, through her efforts, South Carolina was exporting 135,000 pounds of indigo annually.

53 THE EMERGING WOMAN, by the Women's Film Project, n.d. 40 min. b/w. Women's Film Project.

A documentary film about the history of women in the United States. Using old engravings, photographs, newsreels, and other film clips, the filmmakers show the varied economic, social, and cultural experiences of woman, how she felt about her conditions, and how her sex, race, and class often determined her priorities.

54 AN EQUAL CHANCE THROUGH TITLE IX, by American Alliance for Health, Physical Education, and Recreation, 1977. 22 min. color. The Alliance.

Women's Nonprint Media   10

Explains the intent of Title IX and emphasizes the value of sports in a sex-integrated setting.

55 ERA AND THE AMERICAN WAY, by Molly Gregory, 1974. 26 min. color. Serious Business Company.
Produced by the Nevada League of Women Voters, the film shows the various responses to the Equal Rights Amendment by "people in the street."

56 EXPERIMENTS IN FILM: WOMEN, by Jodie Lowe, 1974. 85 min. color. New Line Cinema.
A selection of women's films, including (1) Plumb Line by Carolee Schneemann, (2) Berth of the Big Mamoo by Jody Silver, (3) Road to a Mouse by Pat Sloane, (4) Painting by Pat Sloane, (5) Reticulations by Pat Sloane, (6) Waters Dream by Deborah Dickson, (7) Ordinary Days by Sally Heckle, (8) Actuate, Actuate II, Actuate III by D. Samatowicz, (9) Abstract-Expressionist Movie by Pat Sloane.

57 FACES OF WOMEN, by Les Films Armorial, 1971. 10 min. color. Films Incorporated.
Uses animation to depict various moods of women. Shows the painted woman, woman as Eve, and other images of women in art.

58 FATE OF GUM HUI AND UN HUI, by Newsreel, n.d. 100 min. color. Newsreel.
Shows two possible life styles that a Korean family can face by tracing the story of twin sisters, one in North Korea and one in South Korea. Soundtrack in the Korean language with English subtitles.

59 FEMINISM IN THE CHURCH, by BFC-TV, n.d. 30 min. color. BFC-TV Film Library.
Examines issues of feminism and the church. The women of one church in New York City express their dissatisfaction with the domination of male attitudes and sexist language in religious services. A woman minister in the Methodist Church is interviewed concerning feminism in the church.

60 A FEMINIST SPEAKS, by Brio Films, n.d. 31 min. color. YWCA of Canada.
Canadian sculptor and feminist Maryon Kantaroff discusses the contemporary feminist movement and the situation of women today.

61 FIGHTING BACK, by WNET, 1976. 34 min. color. Indiana University Audiovisual Center.
A report on rape attacks and self protection.

62 FILM FOR MY SON, by Nadja Tesich-Savage, 1975. 28 min. color. Serious Business Company.
   This film was made by the filmmaker to record her child so that one day he might see himself as she experiences him. It is also about the intermingling of memories which their relationship evokes from her--principally, her childhood in rural Yugoslavia during World War II and her early fears of motherhood.

63 THE FLASHETTES, by Bonnie Friedman, 1976. 20 min. color. New Day Films.
   A documentary showing the hopes and aspirations of the young black girls, aged 6-16, who are members of the Flashettes, an inner-city track club from Brooklyn.

64 FORGOTTEN FACES, by University of Southern California, Division of Cinema, 1969. 3 min. color. University of Southern California, Division of Cinema.
   Shows the history of America etched on the faces of its women.

65 FULL CIRCLE: THE WORK OF DORIS CHASE, by Elizabeth Wood, n.d. 10 min. color (also available on videocassette). Perspective Films.
   Shows the sculpture of Doris Chase in its infinite varieties. Some pieces weigh several tons and others, created for dancers, are light enough to move with a gentle touch.

66 GETTING MARRIED, by Charles Braverman Production, 1976. 25 min. color. Pyramid Films.
   Social implications of getting married in America.
   Reviews: Previews, October 1976, p19 ("explores past social and economic pressures for getting married and explains why these may no longer be valid, and in some cases are even causing problems"--John Bennett). Booklist, February 15, 1977, p903.

67 GETTING READY, by Janet Meyers, n.d. 50 min. color. Moonforce Media.
   The story of two young women experiencing the rituals, self-discoveries and pressures of adolescence.

68 GIRLS' SPORTS: ON THE RIGHT TRACK, by Ellen Freyer, 1976. 17 min. color. Phoenix Films.
   Considers the limited opportunities available to women to compete in sporting events. Shows how these limitations are being replaced by new opportunities for women in a variety of competitive sports, including track and field.

69 THE GREAT COVER-UP, by Texture Films, Inc. n.d. 12 min. color. Texture Films, Inc.
A look at clothing as a powerful statement about ourselves, our culture, and our sexuality. In live action and animation, the film makes a number of witty and original observations about dress, from Adam and Eve to today's unisex.

70 GREAT EXPECTATIONS, by the Society for Nutrition Education, 1976. 22 min. color (also available on 3/4" videotape). Society for Nutrition Education.
Valuable information on nutrition for pregnant and nursing women is given by experts in the field of nutrition. The film also portrays women and infants from a variety of social and ethnic backgrounds, concerns and interests.

71 GREAT GRAND MOTHER, by Anne Wheeler and Loma Rasmussen, n.d. 29 min. color. New Day Films.
A history of prairie women. Uses the actual words of women in history to show their struggle to settle and survive in difficult conditions.

72 GRETA'S GIRLS, by Greta Schiller and Thomas Seid, n.d. 18 min. b/w. Women Make Movies, Inc.
The film presents a day in the life of two young women who are first beginning their friendship.

73 HAPPY TO BE ME, by Arthur Mokin Productions, c.1979. 26 min. Arthur Mokin Productions.
A cinematic report of a survey of attitudes of gender roles and gender identity. The survey consists of interviews with students in the public school system of New York City.

74 HARMONY, by Wombat Productions, 1974. 8 min. color. Wombat Productions.
A comic, animated swing at sexual stereotypes.
Review: *Media and Methods*, Ocotober 1975, p74.

75 HEALTHCARING FROM OUR END OF THE SPECULUM, by Women Make Movies, 1976. 32 min. color. Women Make Movies.
An account of women who are beginning to question the quality of health care they receive. Examines the movement for women's self help programs to answer the health needs of women.

76 HOME MOVIE, by Jan Oxenberg, n.d. 12 min. color. Iris Films.
An autobiographical film about lesbianism, combining documentary footage of the lesbian community with actual old home movies of the filmmaker. Personal narration about growing up as a lesbian and coming out.

77 HOMEWARD BOUND: WOMEN IN THE FAMILY IN MINNESOTA HISTORY, by Twin Cities Women's Film Collective, n.d. 28 min. color. Femme Films, Inc.

Explores the variety of family forms and roles Minnesota women have played from the days of Native American predominance to the present.

78 HOOKERS, by Max Scherr, 1975. 25 min. color. Creative Film Society.

Filmed in collaboration with Margo St. James and members of Coyote. The film depicts a number of prostitutes as they see themselves and challenges the moralistic and ideological stereotypes.

79 HOPE IS NOT A METHOD, by Perennial Education, 1976. 16 min. color. Douglas College.

Often using comical animation sequences, the film imparts information on the seven major methods of birth control, and a discussion of vasectomy, tubal ligation and abortion.

80 THE HOUR OF LIBERATION HAS STRUCK, by Newsreel, 1974. 62 min. color. Newsreel.

Through the eyes of a 15-year-old woman, the picture emerges of men and women who have taken up arms and dedicated their life to transforming the conditions of their life in Oman.

81 HOW ABOUT YOU?, by FSM/Pandora Films, n.d. 25 min. b/w. Texture Films, Inc.

Made by three women filmmakers, this film has a pertinent message for young women and young men on birth control and sexuality. Young people are encouraged to take full responsibility for their own sexual lives.

82 HOW WE GOT THE VOTE, by Post-Newsweek Stations, 1976. 55 min. color. Lucern Films.

Presents the story of how women achieved the vote. Review: Landers Film Reviews, November/December 1976, p74 ("The words of Susan B. Anthony and others are repeated in this film and interviews with Dr. Alice Paul ... seem to bridge all the generations of women who gave their time and strength in organizing the National Women's Party to challenge the government for the rights which they believed were theirs").

83 THE HUMAN IMAGE--MASCULINITY/FEMININITY, by the Smithsonian Institution, 1974. 15 min. color. BFA Educational Media.

Identifies and examines common sex-role stereotypes. Discusses the advantages of traditional sex roles and explores the causes for the current redefinition of the traditional roles of men and women.

84 I ONLY WANT YOU TO BE HAPPY, by McGraw-Hill
    Films, 1975. 16 min. color. McGraw-Hill Films.
    A film about a mother and her two daughters and their conflict over expected roles and choices.
    Reviews: Previews, November 1975, p23 ("Though technically sophisticated, its contribution to the discussion of life choices for young women is naive"--Renee Feinberg). Landers Film Reviews, November/December 1975, p74.

85 I'M NOT ONE OF 'EM, by Jan Oxenberg, n.d. 3 min.
    b/w. Iris Films.
    A woman spectator at the roller derby talks about her unique experiences with lesbianism. Hilarious and also painful.

86 IMAGES OF COUNTRY WOMEN: A PATCHWORK QUILT,
    by Lucy Ann Kerry, n.d. 29 min. color. Blue Ridge Films.
    Four women, a secretary, a dairy farmer, a housewife, and an artist talk about their roles and experiences as women in the country. The women are shown at their every-day activities. The portraits explore the consciousness of the women and the society in which they live.

87 IMOGEN CUNNINGHAM AT 93, by CBS News, n.d. 13
    min. color. Carousel Films.
    An interview with the famous photographer.

88 IMOGEN CUNNINGHAM, PHOTOGRAPHER, by American
    Film Institute, 1973. 20 min. color. Time-Life Multi Media.
    The film, through interviews, candid footage of the artist, and a look at her work, expresses the artist's sense of achievement and her vitality and sensitivity.
    Reviews: Media and Methods, December 1975, p66 ("A sensitive, lovingly beautiful portrait of Imogen Cunningham"). Catholic Film, September 30, 1975, p83.

89 IN THE BEST INTERESTS OF THE CHILDREN, by Iris
    Films, 1977. 55 min. color. Iris Films.
    Documentary protrait of eight lesbian mothers, their children, attorneys and social workers; also deals with the issue of child custody problems for lesbians.

90 IT'S NOT ME, by Deborah Wian, 1975. 26 min. color.
    Phoenix Films.
    The film shows the story of Nancy Hohman and her efforts to reclaim her own sense of purpose and identity following an intense emotional crisis.

91 JADE SNOW WONG, by WNET-TV, 1977. 27 min. color
    (also videocassette). Films Incorporated.

The story of a Chinese woman raised in the traditional Chinese way, who struggled to work in order to attain a college education.

92 JANE, by Jon Rosen, 1975. 7 min. color. Jon Rosen.
The limited life style choices as dictated by peers and the media are felt by a young girl.
Review: Previews, January 1977, p13 ("A powerful short film ... provocative"--Renee Feinberg).

93 JUST A MINUTES, by Women Across Canada, 1976. 2 films (6 min. ea.). color. Douglas College.
The first film, "Just a Minutes #1," contains six one-minute films, most of them made by British Columbia women. They are a combination of live action and animation, serious and comic. The second film, "Just a Minutes #2," also is six one-minute films, linked together, made by women from all across Canada.

94 JUST BRIEFLY, by Louis Fleming, 1976. 15 min. b/w. Phoenix Films.
A young black woman's search for emotional fulfillment.

95 KAREN: WOMEN IN SPORTS, by Marion Barling, 1976. 15 min. color. Women in Focus.
Documents a young girl's fight for acceptance by her peers and her local Soccer League.

96 KILLING US SOFTLY: ADVERTISING'S IMAGE OF WOMEN, by Jean Kilbourne, 1978. 30 min. color. Cambridge Documentary Films.
Using ads from magazines, newspapers, album covers and storefront windows, the filmmaker has produced a concise analysis of a $40 billion industry that preys on the fears and insecurities of the American consumer. Other issues raised are the objectification of women, the exploitation of sexuality, the caricaturing of femininity and masculinity, the tyranny of "ideal" beauty, and the glorification of violence against women.

97 LABOR, by Josie Ramstad, 1976. 3 min. color. silent. Serious Business Company.
The birth experience is told from the mother's point of view in this animated film drawn from the filmmaker's real life experience.

98 LEADERS IN AMERICAN MEDICINE--GRACE A. GOLDSMITH, M.D., by National Medical Audiovisual Center, 1974. 58 min. color. National Audiovisual Center.
Presents an interview with Dr. Goldsmith who discusses her interest in nutritional and metabolic diseases.

Recalls her research on drugs and diet and her work on vitamins which led to the establishment of minimum daily requirements.

99 LEADERS IN AMERICAN MEDICINE--HELEN B. TAUS-
    SIG, M.D., by National Medical Audiovisual Center,
    1973. 50 min. b/w. National Audiovisual Center.
    Dr. Taussig describes her medical education at John Hopkins, where she was the first woman to be appointed a full professor. Discusses her pediatric internship, her interest in congenital heart deformations, and her research on pediatric malformations due to the use of Thalidomide which led to her warning American officials of the dangers of the drugs.

100 LEARNING TO READ BETWEEN THE STEREOTYPES,
    by Maria Armour, n.d. 20 min. color. YWCA of
    Canada.
    The film raises some fundamental questions about the treatment of sex roles in many of the materials used in schools. Assumptions made about female and male children and adults in educational materials are examined. Suggestions are made as to how teachers can deal with these limiting and potentially damaging stereotypes.
    Review: Media and Methods, October 1975, p73.

101 LIFE AND DEATH OF FRIDA KAHLO, by Karen Crom-
    mie and David Crommie, 1976. 40 min. color.
    Serious Business Company.
    A documentary of the life of Mexico's most famous woman painter, Frida Kahlo.
    Review: Ms., October 1976, p112.

102 LIKE A ROSE, by Tomatoe Productions, Inc., 1975.
    23 min. color. b/w. Tomatoe Productions, Inc.
    Focuses on the lonely and frustrating existence of two women currently serving 25-year sentences in the Missouri State Penitentiary.
    Review: Media Report to Women, December 1976, p2.

103 LINDA'S FILM: MENSTRUATION, by Linda Feferman,
    1974. 18 min. color. Phoenix Films.
    The film exposes the myths and old wives' tales long surrounding menstruation. An animated segment explains the physiological process of menstruation.
    Reviews: Preview, March 1976, p36 ("light-hearted presentation of misconceptions, anxieties, and social confusion about menstruation"--Maude T. Parker). Booklist, April 1, 1975, p797. EFLA Evaluations, 1975, p8898. Landers Film Reviews, May 1975, p300.

104 LOOKING AT TOMORROW...WHAT WILL SHE CHOOSE?, by Susan Shippey, 1975. 16 min. color. Churchill Films.
Congresswoman Yvonne Burke introduces seven young, self-reliant women each at a rewarding job. Explores the process of choosing and preparing as well as the sense of fulfillment in the job.
Reviews: Previews, September 1975, p14. Landers Film Reviews, November/December 1975, p77.

105 LORRAINE HANSBERRY: THE BLACK EXPERIENCE IN THE CREATION OF DRAMA, by Films for the Humanities, 1975. 35 min. color. Films for the Humanities.
Presents the writer's artistic growth and her unique vision largely in her own words and her own voice. The film shows how Ms. Hansberry's talent developed from her own experiences and those of her people in fashioning a dramatic view point which has made her work endure.
Reviews: Previews, December 1975, p16. Booklist, October 15, 1975, p310. Media and Methods, October 1975, p74. Landers Film Reviews, January/February 1976, p136.

106 LOVE IS LIKE A FOOL: A FILM ABOUT MALVINA REYNOLDS, by Red Hen Films, 1977. 28 min. color. Red Hen Films.
The songwriter, folksinger and political activist performs and provokes at the age of 76. The film shows Malvina as she composes, records an album, performs in concert, rehearses, and manages her record and publishing companies.

107 LUCY COVINGTON: NATIVE AMERICAN INDIAN, by Odyssey Productions. 16 min. color. Encyclopaedia Britannica.
Documentary film of the active leader and spokesperson for the Colville Indians of Northern Washington.

108 MADSONG, by Kathleen Laughlin, 1976. 5 min. color. Serious Business Company.
Explores childbirth, sexual bonding between man and woman, and tug of war between mother and child. Uses natural photography, animation, optical printing, and mulitple voices.

109 MAHALIA JACKSON, by Jules Victor Schwerin, 1974. 34 min. color. Phoenix Films.
A portrait of Mahalia Jackson who spread the religious music of American blacks from the congregations in small churches to the vast audiences of concert halls and the mass media.

Women's Nonprint Media   18

110 MAKING IT, by Pat Corbett, 1975. 18 min. color.
        Moreland-Latchford Productions.
    Janis and Brian's relationship breaks up over differing sexual values. The film shows the two discussing their relationship and their insights into what makes for a fulfilling mature relationship.
        Review: Media and Methods, December 1976, p20.

111 MANY GIFTS, ONE SPIRIT, by National Council of
        Churches, n.d. 30 min. color. National Council of
        Churches.
    Changing attitudes about sex roles in society are affecting the life of the church as well. The film gives an overview of the Assembly of the United Methodist Women in Cincinnati (October 4-7, 1973). Leaders reflect upon the kinds of roles women will be calling for themselves to play in the contemporary church.

112 A MATTER OF CHOICE, by Maria Armour, n.d. 10
        min. color. YWCA of Canada.
    The film illustrates the ways in which society treats boys and girls differently so that they grow up with different goals and aspirations. Facts such as employment wage statistics are used to prove the point.

113 MAXINE, by Sarah Snider, 1975. 13 min. b/w. Iris
        Films.
    A documentary portrait of a woman who is dying, isolated in her rural home with her husband and two sons --an eloquent celebration of a woman who, although her body fails her, remains strong.

114 MENSES, by Barbara Hammer, 1973. 4 min. color.
        Iris Films.
    A wry film on the disagreeable aspects of menstruation combining both the imagery and politics of the subject.

115 MISS, MRS. OR MS.--WHAT'S IT ALL ABOUT?, by
        CBS News, n.d. 25 min. color. Carousel Films.
    A report on how the term "Ms." has become an established part of our vocabulary. The stereotyping of traditional roles for boys and girls are discussed by news correspondents Sylvia Chase and Christopher Glenn.

116 MUJER DE MILFUEGAS (WOMAN OF A THOUSAND
        FIRES), by Chick Strand, 1976. 15 min. color.
        Serious Business Company.
    A portrait of a Latin American woman who typifies the consciousness of women in rural parts of such countries as Spain, Greece and Mexico.

117 MUSEREEL #1:   TAPESTRY OF WOMAN-SPIRIT, by

Denise Bostrum, Carol Clement, Ariel Dougherty, Nancy Peck, and Marilyn Ries, n.d. 17 min. color. Women Make Movies, Inc.

A documentary of the first women's spirituality conference, Through the Looking Glass: A Gynergenetic Experience, in Boston, 1976. Combines live action, still photographs, animation and drawings.

118 MY PEOPLE ARE MY HOME, by Twin Cities Women's Film Collective, 1976. 60 min. color. Insight Exchange.

Bicentennial project of the Collective draws from the experiences of Midwestern women born around 1900--women of farms and prairies, factory women, native American Women--to create a document of women's history.

119 NANA: UN PORTRAIT, by Jamil Simon. 25 min. color. (In French with English subtitles.) Third Eye Films.

Offers a classic Old-World view of womanhood that contrasts sharply with the role of women in today's society. Eighty-year-old Louise Zikha reviews the highlights of her life that began in Baghdad, steeped in the centuries-old traditions of Jewish family life.

120 NINJA, by Christine Mohanna, n.d. 25 min. b/w. Moonforce Media.

The story of a lesbian who lives out her dream of becoming a Samurai.

121 NO LIES, by Mitchell Block, 1973. 16 min. color. Phoenix Films.

A study of a young woman's reaction to her rape.
Review: Landers Film Reviews, January 1975, p161. ("The film, winner of numerous awards, is powerful in its presentation ... an extraordinary statement.")

122 NOT A PRETTY PICTURE, by Martha Coolidge, 1975. 83 min. color. Martha Coolidge.

Explores events surrounding the filmmaker's rape while in boarding school and its effects on her.
Review: Ms., July 1976, p39.

123 OLGA: A FILM PORTRAIT, by John Seppard, 1975. 47 min. color. Carousel Films.

Biographical study of Russian gymnast, Olga Korbut. Shows the routine which earned her gold medals in the 1972 Olympics.
Reviews: Previews, May 1976, p32 ("will be of special interest to those interested in gymnastics as a sport"--Laura Smith). Booklist, December 1975, p520. Sightlines, Fall 1975, p13.

124 ON A COLD AFTERNOON, by Barbara Jabaily/Women's Interart Center, n.d. 8 min. b/w. Moonforce Media.
Two women who deal with their attraction for each other in different ways are the subjects of this short drama.

125 ONE WOMAN, by Ann Wheeler, 1972. 23 min. color. Douglas College.
The film shows two days in the life of a young middle-class woman who is leaving her marriage. The financial, emotional, and social circumstances a woman must face when she sets out on her own are depicted realistically.

126 OTHER WOMEN, OTHER WORK, by Churchill Films, n.d. 20 min. color. Churchill Films.
Vignettes of a number of women doing unusual jobs and doing away with the myth of "woman's work."

127 OUR LITTLE MUNCHKIN HERE, by Lois Tupper, 1975. 12 min. color. Iris Films.
A painful episode in the life of an adolescent girl who finds herself at odds with her family environment.

128 PATCHWORK QUILT, by Kim Ondaatji, 1974. 11 min. color. YWCA of Canada.
Shows Canadian women actively engaged in imaginative, highly skilled handwork.

129 PEACE WOMEN, by CBS News, n.d. 16 min. color. Carousel Films.
Portrays the two Irish women, Betty Williams and Mairead Corrigan, and their organization "Peace People," devoted to a nonviolent solution to the Irish civil war.

130 PEGGY GUGGENHEIM: ART IN VENICE, by Mondadori, 1975. 44 min. color. Films for the Humanities.
Peggy Guggenheim conducts us on a memorable journey into the art history of the past and the present. She emerges as a patron who has literally mothered modern art with her depth of understanding and insight.
Review: *Previews*, May 1976, p17.

131 PERIOD PIECE, by Emily Culpepper, n.d. 10 min. color. Insight Exchange.
Introduction to menstruation. A far cry from the traditional clinical introduction. The film playfully pokes fun at the idea of menstruation as a handicap.

132 PICTURES, by Janet Benn, n.d. 3 min. color. Women Make Movies, Inc.
An animated film made to commemorate International Woman's Year.

133 A PRIDE IN BELONGING, by United States Office of Information for the Armed Forces, 1975. 28 min. color. National Audiovisual Center.
   Depicts the changing role of women and occupations available for women in today's military. Presents women discussing the benefits of life in the military and the changes that have taken place.

134 QUIET REVOLUTION OF MRS. HARRIS, by Lore Caulfield, 1976. 20 min. color. Doubleday Multi Media.
   Explores the concepts of individual freedom, opportunity, and choice with regard to the rights of women and minority groups.
   Review: Landers Film Reviews, November/December 1976, p83.

135 QUILTING WOMEN, by Elizabeth Barrett/Appalshop. n.d. 28 min. color.
   Shows the traditional art of quiltmaking from the process of piecing to the quilting bee.

136 RAPE CULTURE, by Cambridge Documentary Films, n.d. 35 min. color. Cambridge Documentary Films.
   The film examines popular films, advertising, music, and "adult entertainment" and records the insights of rapists, victims, rape crisis workers, authors and prisoners.

137 REMEDIOS VARO, by Jomi Garcia Ascot, 1976. 20 min. color. Serious Business Company.
   Using images from her paintings, the film captures the sense of otherworldliness created in the paintings of this Mexican surrealist (1913-1963).

138 REVELATIONS: ULLA, by Amelia Anderson, 1971. 4 min. color. Creative Film Society.
   Features model Ulla Anderson Jones. In a dramatization revealed to herself in a dream, Ulla peels the many-layered roles she has acquired in society enabling her to recognize her existence in the consciousness of her soul. Vignettes bare relationships to mother, father, grandmother, girlfriend, lover and child.

139 ROOKIE OF THE YEAR, by Daniel Wilson, 1976. 47 min. color. Time-Life Multi Media.
   Shows the problems faced by a young girl who joins a Little League baseball team. She finds opposition from all sides--her teammates, her brother, her girlfriends, parents of teammates, and coaches of opposing teams.

140 ROSE ARGOFF, by WNET-TV, n.d. 9 min. b/w. Carousel Films.

A study of the aging. Argoff, a 75-year-old retired woman, describes her life in America after she emigrated from Russia.

141 ROSI, by Rachel Wohl, 1976. 9 min. color. Serious Business Company.
Work aboard a Massachusetts fishing trawler has traditionally been off-limits to women, but Rosi hauls beside the men, it being apparent that the catch is more important than the discrimination. A sensitive portrait of a woman and her perceptions of the inner and outer aspects of her personality.

142 RUTH STOUT'S GARDEN, by Arthur Mokin, 1975. 23 min. color. Arthur Mokin Productions.
An interview with a 90-year-old woman who has a great deal to offer on subjects ranging from her vegetable garden to growing old.
Reviews: Previews, November 1975, p1 ("Recommended for junior high through college, and public libraries, with a clientele requesting material on gardening, ecology, natural living, natural foods, and women's studies" --Peter Milbury). Media and Methods, December 1975, p68.

143 SHADOW PLAY, by Peggie Chute, 1975. 38 min. color. Creative Film Society.
A dramatization of the plight of the single girl as she is programmed by society to seek out and find the ideal male companion.

144 SIMPLEMENTE JENNY, by the Women's Film Project, c.1978. 33 min. color. Women's Film Project.
A film about women in Latin America and the cultural values that shape their lives. It is a film about the models of society and the facts of poverty and violence. It focuses on three adolescent girls in a reformatory in Bolivia.

145 SO WHERE'S MY PLACE ALREADY?, by Reelfeelings, 1976. 20 min. color. Douglas College.
The film is a romantic fantasy done in the style of a black soap opera. It follows the experiences of a young girl, who believes in all those "Hollywood dreams" as she tries to fulfill her fantasies in catching a man and marriage.

146 SOME AMERICAN FEMINISTS, by the National Film Board of Canada, c.1979. 56 min. Arthur Mokin Productions.
The film consists of interviews with some of the leaders of the American feminist movement--Ti-Grace Atkinson, Rita Mae Brown, Betty Friedan, Margo Jefferson, Lila Karp, and Kate Millet--discussing past, present and prospects for the movement.

147 THE SOONER THE BETTER, by Jamil Simon Productions, 1977. 27 min. color. Third Eye Films.
Filmed at multiethnic preschools around the country, it illustrates the essentials of a nonsexist classroom, and describes and demonstrates specific teaching ideas aimed at expanding horizons for both boys and girls.
Reviews: Ms., February 1978. Film News/Learning Resources, January/February 1978. Baby Talk, January 1978. London Daily Mail, January 18, 1978. Newsday, January 25, 1978.

148 SUFFRAGISTS: A CENTURY LATER, by Blue Eyes Productions, n.d. 15 min. color. YWCA of Canada.
Film of a round table discussion by some of Canada's leading women's rights activists. Many major issues in the women's rights movement are discussed. They look at women's expectations and at whether the women's rights movement has accomplished anything during a century.

149 SUGAR AND SPIKES, by Odeon Films, 1974. 32 min. color. Odeon Films.
Includes comments by parents, teachers, coaches, and students about the participation of women in high school and college sports.

150 SYLVIA, FRAN AND JAY, by Churchill Films, n.d. 25 min. b/w. Churchill Films.
Three young women voice their feelings about the role of wife-mother-housekeeper: Sylvia who shares responsibilities with her husband, Fran in transition, Jay the traditionalist.

151 TEENAGE MOTHER: A BROKEN DREAM, by CBS News, n.d. 15 min. color. Carousel Films.
Examines the life of a 15-year-old unwed mother. Presents the stark picture of the 900,000 teenagers who become pregnant, drop out of school and end up on welfare every year.

152 THAT'S OUR BABY, by Carrie Agins and Jack Agins, 1975. 23 min. color. Serious Business Company.
The film presents childbirth as a natural and rewarding event in which fear may be diminished through education and preparation.
Review: Landers Film Reviews, November/December 1975, p91.

153 THEY ARE THEIR OWN GIFTS, by Lucille Rhodes and Margaret Murphy, n.d. 3 films (approx. 18 min. each). color. New Day Films.
Portraits of three famous artists. Part 1--Muriel Rukeyser, poet; Part 2--Anna Sokolow, choreographer; Part 3--Alice Neel, painter.

154 THREE, by Grove Press, 1976. 18 min. color. Grove Press.
Interviews with three women are used to explore the subject of bisexuality in women.
Review: Previews, January 1977, p8 ("valuable motivational device for the serious students of the range of human sexual behavior"--Maude Parker).

155 THREE GUESSES, by The National Film Board of Canada, 1973. 29 min. color. Phoenix Films.
The many roles that one assumes as an individual are shown in this study of Jackie Burroughs--actress, mother, woman, girl, daughter, estranged wife.
Review: Landers Film Review, January 1975, p164 ("A good discussion starter on choices of life style and individual values").

156 THE TIME HAS COME, by Jamil Simon, 1977. 22 min. color. Third Eye Films.
Explores the simple elements of a nonsexist home environment and also deals with influences outside the home such as television and school.
Reviews: Ms., Februrary, 1978. Film News/Learning Resources, January/February 1978. Baby Talk, January 1978. London Daily Mail, January 18, 1978. Newsday, January 25, 1978.

157 TIME HAS NO SYMPATHY, by Kristine Samuelson, 1975. 28 min. color. Serious Business Company.
A portrait of women in prison. The film gives detailed coverage of daily prison life and examines the feelings and needs of women prisoners. Special attention is given to the problems of mothers separated from their children.

158 UNION MAIDS, by Julie Reichert, James Klein, Miles Mogulesen, n.d. 48 min. b/w. New Day Films.
Three women in their sixties tell the way things really were back in the thirties, when people risked their jobs and their lives to organize trade unions. The film intercuts the stories of the three women with newsreels of labor struggles to illustrate an almost forgotten part of American history.
Reviews: Sevendays, March 4, 1977, p42-43 ("the film has great merit. It is easy to forget the bloody struggles carried on just for the right to organize, and we seldom think of women as part of that struggle"--Rosalyn Baxandall). Film News, November/December 1976, p20.

159 VALERIE, by Nafasi Productions, 1975. 15 min. color. Phoenix Films.
Explores some of the attitudes and insights of the

sculptor, Valerie Maynard, whose work is acclaimed in America and abroad.

160 THE VANISHING MOMMY, by NBC, 1977. 25 min. color. Films Incorporated.
Examines the question of working mothers--why they work, the problems they face at home and on the job, and the effects on the children.

161 THE VISIBLE WOMAN, by Beryl Fox, n.d. 30 min. color, b/w. YWCA of Canada.
A film about the history of women and women's rights in Canada.

162 EL VISITANTE (THE VISITATION), by Texture Films, 1975. 9 min. b/w. Texture Films.
A portrait of a woman who feels trapped and unfulfilled in the monotony of her daily life as a wife and mother.
Reviews: Previews, December 1975, p21 ("In our changing society when the traditional role of women is being challenged, [this film] is vitally needed"--Milena Pribramska). Landers Film Reviews, January/February 1976, p122.

163 W.O.W. (WOMEN OF THE WORLD), by Faith Hubley, 1975. 11 min. color. Pyramid Films.
An animated view of human history from a feminist perspective. Emphasizes the evaluation of women's role in civilization.
Reviews: Sightlines, Fall 1975, p14 ("Symbolism is somewhat heavy-handed, but the film serves as a good introduction for women's programs"--Carol Emmens). Media and Methods, December 1976, p17. Ms., October 1976, p111.

164 WAYS OF SEEING, by John Berger for BBC-TV, n.d. Film 1, 18 min. Film 2, 12 min. color. Douglas College.
In the first film Berger considers the ways the men have seen women in the past and how this has influenced the way that women see themselves today. The second film is a discussion among Berger and five women about the implications of the women's self image.
Review: Wilson Library Bulletin, January 1975, p350.

165 WE ARE WOMAN, by Avanti Films, 1975. 29 min. color. University of California Extension Media Center.
The film uses interviews and graphic artwork to trace the economic, social, and historic factors that have determined the traditional role of women. Stresses the needs for individual rights for men as well as women.
Reviews: Media Mix, April 1975, p3 ("does point out the injustices committed against women and explains

them by giving the history of traditional sex roles"). Mass Media, November 10, 1975, p3. Media and Methods, October 1975, p74.

166 WE WILL NOT BE BEATEN, by Transition House Films, 1978. 41 min. b/w. Transition House Films.
The film was made at Transition House, a Boston area shelter for battered women. Women discuss their experiences and their difficulties in trying to escape a battering situation.

167 A WEDDING IN THE FAMILY, by Debra Frames, n.d. 22 min. color. New Day Films.
The film presents diverse viewpoints about marriage, careers, and women's roles.

168 WE'RE ALIVE, by Women's Film Workshop of UCLA and the Video Workshop of California Institution for Women, n.d. 45 min. color, b/w. Insight Exchange.
Thoughts and feelings of women inside California Institution for Women. The film is the result of eight months of collective effort by women both within and outside the prison. Prisoners discuss their lives, sexuality, and methods of survival. Informs about law and punishment in California, with facts on drugs, racism, recidivism and the indeterminate sentence.

169 WHAT 80 MILLION WOMEN WANT, by Unique Film Company, 1972. 55 min. b/w. silent. Film Classic Exchange.
Uses a drama featuring Emmeline Pankhurst to present the cause of woman suffrage. The film has English subtitles.

170 WHAT MAKES MILLIE RUN?, by Brigham Young University, 1976. 16 min. color. Brigham Young University.
Physical fitness for women.

171 WIFE BEATING, by NBC, 1977. 27 min. color (videocassette also). Films Incorporated.
A film exploring the problem of wife-beating, just now emerging as a serious social problem.

172 WISHFULFILMING, by Santa Cruz Women's Media Collective, n.d. 13 min. b/w. Women's Film Coop.
A documentary about a collective of women coming together to make a film and finally deciding to make a film about themselves making a film. The work explores the process of working together collectively and the struggle to develop new forms of nonhierarchical organization.

173 WITH BABIES AND BANNERS: STORY OF THE WOMEN'S EMERGENCY BRIGADE, by Lorraine Gray, Anne Bohlen, Lyn Goldfarb, n.d. 45 min. color. New Day Films.

The story of the Women's Emergency Brigade of the C.I.O.'s Great General Motors sit down strike in Flint, Michigan, in 1937.

174 WITH JUST A LITTLE TRUST, by Teleketics, 1975. 15 min. color. University of California Extension Media Center.

Portrayal of a woman with children who must cope with the bureaucratic red tape and dehumanizing requirements of the welfare system.

175 WOMAN CANDIDATE, by Lucy Ann Kerry, n.d. 13 min. color. Blue Ridge Films.

The film is about Flora Crater, the first woman to run for a statewide office in Virginia. We follow her on her campaign for lieutenant governor. She discusses the role of women in politics today and the special problems a woman faces as a candidate.

176 WOMAN IS, by Sandy Ostertag, 1975. 12 min. color. Phoenix Films.

Explores the history and character of roles women occupy in society. Images of women from drawings, paintings and photographs illustrate the situation of women today and throughout history.

177 WOMAN POWER: A WOMAN'S PLACE, by United Nations Television, 1975. 28 min. color. United Nations Radio and Visual Services.

Filmed in Sweden, the film brings the Swedish experiment to life. Shows the effects of the educational system's attempt to end sex stereotyping. Depicts the efforts to give substance to the words of equality.

Reviews: Film Library Quarterly, Vol #2 1976 pp54-55 ("will be of value as long as equality for women continues to be a vital issue"--Madeline Friedlander). Sightlines, Fall 1975, p14.

178 WOMAN TO WOMAN, by Donna Deitch, n.d. 48 min. color. Moonforce Media.

A documentary about hookers, housewives, and mothers which combines historical footage with contemporary interviews.

179 WOMAN: WHO IS ME?, by Tricipts Production, 1977. 11 min. color. Serious Business Company.

The film examines the persistance of myths about women through the ages. An analysis and evaluation of the stereotypical roles and images of women.

180 A WOMAN'S PLACE IS IN THE HOUSE: A PORTRAIT OF ELAINE NOBLE, by WGBH Educational Foundation, 1975. 30 min. color. WGBH Educational Foundation.
Follows the typical day of a radical lesbian elected to the Massachusetts legislature in 1974.

181 WOMEN, by OECA, 1973. 30 min. color. Films Inc.
A dramatic portrayal of George Bernard Shaw's relationship with women. In his life, as well as in his plays, Shaw was an early advocate of women's liberation.

182 WOMEN AGAINST RAPE: SIX PUBLIC SERVICE ANNOUNCEMENTS, by Pamela Stephan, 1976. 6 Films. (30 min. ea.). color. Serious Business Company.
These six Public Service Announcements provide vital information for rape victims and produce support for rape prevention/crisis centers.

183 WOMEN AT WORK: CHANGE, CHOICE, CHALLENGE, by Encyclopaedia Britannica, n.d. 19 min. color. Encyclopaedia Britannica.
Dialogue with seven women--an oil worker, a nurse, a jockey, a locomotive engineer, a surgeon, a judge, and a candidate for Congress. Reveals their attitudes about work, their personal roles and shows the differing views of their work-family-community relationships.

184 WOMEN EMERGING: COMPARING CULTURAL EXPECTATIONS, by Far West Laboratory for Educational Research and Development, 1975. 27 min. b/w. University of California Extension Media Center.
Documents the experiences of a multicultural women's class in an experimental high school. Shows how work in the class helped class members confront and understand stereotyped perceptions of sex roles.

185 WOMEN I LOVE, by Barbara Hammer, n.d. 23 min. color. Moonforce Media.
A lesbian's celebration of five friends and lovers.

186 WOMEN IN COMMUNICATIONS, by Forum Productions, 1975. 15 min. color. BFA Educational Media.
The film shows a freelance camera person making a film about two other women, one a newspaper reporter and the other a disc jockey.
Reviews: Previews, March 1976, p26 ("The purpose is to depict women in communications successfully coping with traditionally male roles"--Douglas Elwell). Forecast for Home Economics, September 1975, pF-36.

187 WOMEN IN MANAGEMENT: THREAT OR OPPORTUN-

ITY?, by CRM Films Incorporated, 1975. 30 min. color. McGraw-Hill Films.

The film examines the stereotyped images of women in administrative and managerial positions.

Review: Previews, September 1976, p17 ("seems to be aimed at a male audience, and as such would be very useful in a work shop situation"--Margie Schoemberg).

188 WOMEN OF TELECOMMUNICATIONS STATION #6, by Newsreel, n.d. 20 min. b/w. Newsreel.

Young North Vietnamese women learning the skills to operate a vital communication and relay station and defend it against attack. Touches on personal aspects of women's lives and their transformation from a role of bondage to one of full participation in their country's struggle. Made by North Vietnamese with English soundtrack.

189 WOMEN OF THE RHONDDA, by London Women's Film Group, 1973. 20 min. b/w. Women's Film Coop.

In the Rhondda Valley of Wales, a mining district, three women share their lives, and the lives of their mothers, as slaves of slaves. The film describes how the women's work is the underpining of an entire system of exploitation.

190 WOMEN OF THE TOUBAU, by Anne Balfour-Fraser, 1975. 25 min. color. Phoenix Films.

The Toubau are a nomadic people living within the Sahara. Toubau women are treated as equals by the men and share every aspect of life. The film documents the life style of the people.

Reviews: Booklist, December 15, 1974, p414. Landers Film Reviews, September/October 1975, p40. Sightlines, Fall 1975, p15.

191 WOMENCENTERING, by Nancy Peck, n.d. 8 min. b/w. Women Make Movies, Inc.

Portrays a young mother's first interest in feminism.

192 WOMEN'S BASKETBALL--JUMPBALL, by BFA Educational Media, 1976. 15 min. color. BFA Educational Media.

An introductory film on competitive women's basketball.

Review: Previews, March 1977, p6 ("exciting film wth good action sequences that could motivate teams to better utilization of the basic skills of basketball"--Cynthia Getsinger).

193 WOMEN"S TRACK AND FIELD, by The Athletic Institute, 1976. 4 films (20 min. ea.). color. The Athletic Institute.

The four films are entitled Fundamentals of Running, The Running Events, The Throwing Events, and The Jumping Events.

194 THE WORKING MOTHERS SERIES, by Kathleen Shannon, n.d. 10 films. color. Douglas College.

The films are discussions with a number of Canadian women from a wide range of cultural backgrounds and economic classes. (1) It's Not Enough (15 min.)--working women in Canada, (2) Mothers Are People (7 min.)--problems of daycare for children of working women, (3) Tiger on a Tight Leash (7 min.)--problems of a professional woman in finding adequate daycare for her children, (4) Would I Ever Like to Work (8 min.)--interview with a welfare mother with seven children, (5) Our Dear Sisters (15 min.)--women's support for other women, (6) Luckily I Need a Little Sleep (7 min.)--interview with a woman who works and who is also expected to do all the care of the home and family, (7) Extensions of the Family (14 min.)--members of a communal house discuss their sharing of childcare and housework, (8) They Appreciate You More (14 min.)--interview with middle class family discussing changes in family due to a working mother, (9) Like the Trees (14 min.)--interview with a Metis woman, her experiences as a minority group in society, (10) The Spring and Fall of Nina Polanski (6 min.)--an animated film making a statement about motherhood in paintings and sounds.

Review: Ms., October 1975, p111 ("The candor and warmth of each interview are catalysts for discussion"--Carol Emmens).

195 WOULD I EVER LIKE TO WORK, by Kathleen Shannon/ National Film Board of Canada, n.d. 9 min. color. Moonforce Media.

An interview with a welfare mother of nine.

196 THE WRITERS IN AMERICA: A FILM SERIES, by Robert O. Moore, c.1977. Perspective Films.

Eight portraits of a group of writers whose achievements have influenced our national culture.
1. Eudora Welty, 29 min., color.
2. Toni Morrison, 28 min., color.
3. John Gardner, 29 min., color.
4. Robert Duncan, 29 min., color.
5. Muriel Rukeyser, 28 min., color.
6. Janet Flanner (Genét), 29 min., color.
7. Ross MacDonald, 29 min., color.
8. Wright Morris, 29 min., color.
(Also available on video cassette.)

Eudora Welty: "each story teaches me how to write it, but not how to write the one afterwards." Toni Morrison: "The writing was something I did with relief. It was a way of ordering, I think, the universe." Muriel

Rukeyser: "People think it's easy to make a point."
Janet Flanner (Genét): "I was fortunate in having been gifted enough for writing to have turned to it and to have clamped onto it, to have attached myself to writing like a limpet."

197 THE YELLOW WALLPAPER, by Marie Ashton, n.d. 14 min. color. Women Make Movies, Inc.
   The film, based on a book by Charlotte Perkins Gilman, is the story of a Victorian woman rebelling against her predestined societal role and desperately battling to maintain her sanity.

198 YOUNG WOMEN IN SPORTS, by BFA Educational Media, 1974. 15 min. color. BFA Educational Material.
   Shows four high school athletes performing and talking about training and competing in track and field, gymnastics, and swimming.

199 YOUR MOVE, by National Film Board of Canada, 1976. 22 min. color. Films Incorporated.
   Myths and taboos that have prevented women from participating in sports.

200 YUDI, by Mirra Bank, n.d. 20 min. b/w. New Day Films.
   A portrait of an older woman who describes her life and growing up on New York's Lower East Side.

VIDEOTAPES

201 ABORTION, by the Vancouver Status of Women Commission, 1975. 30 min. b/w. Douglas College.
   The practical and legal aspects of abortion are discussed in an interview with a woman lawyer and a woman from the Vancouver Women's Health Collective.

202 ABORTION, by Francis Wyland/Women's Involvement Program, 1973. 24 min. b/w. Women's Involvement Program.
   Surveys the history of abortion practices, attitudes, and the law. Discusses current techniques of abortion and the importance of women's rights to control their bodies.

203 THE ADVOCATES, by WGBH-TV, 1978. 59 min. color. Public Television Library.
   A debate on "Should the Equal Rights Amendment Be Ratified?" Witnesses in favor of ratification include Barbara Babcock, Assistant U.S. Attorney General, and Eleanor Smeal, president of the National Organization for Women. Arguing against are Phyllis Schlafly, president of the Stop ERA Organization.

204 AGE IS A WOMEN'S ISSUE, by WNED-TV, 1977. 29 min. color. Public Television Library.
   Tish Sommers, Co-Coordinator of NOW's Task Force on Older Women, discusses how age discrimination affects the older woman.

205 AGE IS BECOMING, by WNED-TV, 1977. 29 min. color. Public Television Library.
   Lydia Bragger of the Grey Panthers, Marjory Collins, editor of the magazine Prime Time, and Tish Sommers of NOW's Task Force on Older Women discuss their work to change the image of aging as well as the advantages of growing older and what to do about the disadvantages.

206 AGE IS MONEY BLUES, by WNED-TV, 1977. 29 min. color. Public Television Library.
   Laurie Shields of the Alliance of Displaced Homemakers. and Tish Sommers of NOW's Task Force on Older Women, describe the "Displaced Homemakers Bill"--a proposed self-help program for women who have been homemakers and are being excluded from the job market by age discrimination.

Videotapes

207 ALICE, WHO DID THAT TO YOUR FACE? A STUDY OF BATTERED WOMEN, by University of Windsor, n.d. 55 min. color. Satellite Video Exchange Society.
Interviews with battered women, their husbands and people on the street. Shows how the law is unsupportive of battered women. Women who work with transition houses are also interviewed.

208 ARVILLA, by WMHT-TV, 1977. 29 min. color. Public Television Library.
A portrait of Arvilla Groesbeck, a 63-year-old woman dairy farmer, struggling to survive in an occupation where male dominance is still unchallenged. She talks about her life, politics, and economic problems.

209 THE BALLOON LADY, by Focus, 1975. 60 min. b/w. Satellite Video Exchange Society.
Deals with women's property rights after marriage and contains a dramatized account of a woman's fight for property after her divorce.

210 THE BATTERED WIFE, by Interaction, 1975. 33 min. b/w. Satellite Video Exchange Society.
About wife-beating and divorce. The laws about divorce and wife-beating are examined and a drama of a court divorce case is presented.

211 BATTERED WOMEN, by Spectra Feminist Media, n.d. Valle Jones/Spectra Feminist Media. [No data avail.]

212 BETTY KAPLOWITZ--BLUES SINGER, by Women in Focus, 1975. 30 min. color. Women in Focus.
Betty Kaplowitz gives a dynamic and powerful rendering of the blues, including several of her compositions. She talks about her life in San Francisco and accompanies her singing with guitar playing.

213 BIRTH CONTROL, by Francis Wyland, 1973. 33 min. b/w. Women's Involvement Program, c/o Francis Wyland.
A study of the female reproduction system and methods of birth control. Original graphics.

214 BIRTH OF LUDI, by Steve and Liz Grumette, 1974. 43 min. b/w. Satellite Video Exchange Society.
Documentary of the attitudes and lifestyle of a women who decides to have her baby born at home.

215 BREAST CANCER UPDATE, by WNED-TV, 1977. 29 min. color. Public Television Library.
Rose Krushner, author of the book Breast Cancer: A Personal History and an Investigative Report, explores the controversy over the use of mammography in cancer detec-

Women's Nonprint Media 34

tion, the risk factors for breast cancer, and the development of the "phantom breast" for the testing of X-ray equipment.

216 BREAST SELF-EXAMINATION, by Barbara Steinman, 1975. 25 min. b/w. Satellite Video Exchange Society.
At the Women's Health Collective in Vancouver a group learns how to examine breasts for early signs of tumors.

217 BY THEMSELVES, by University of California Extension Media Center, 1977. 34 min. b/w. University of California Extension Media Center.
Portrait of three single women, one divorced, one widowed, and one unmarried, who discuss solitude, careers, and personal encounters.

218 CAROLINE HERSCHEL: ASTRONOMER 1750-1848, by Women in Focus, 1977. 32 min. color. Women in Focus.
A historical dramatization of the life of Caroline Herschel, an important scientist of the 18th century. Based upon her memoirs and correspondence, the tape shows the relationship between the material conditions of an 18th-century woman's life and her work as a scientist.

219 CARTOONISTS LEE MARRS AND TRINA, by Suzanne C. Fox, 1975. 30 min. color. Suzanne C. Fox.
Traces the history of women in comics and examines two Bay Area women comic editors' publishing efforts and experiences.
Review: California Video Resource Project Patch Panel, January/February 1976, p18 ("Useful not only as a discussion/starter for women's programs, this tape would be effective in a program on comics as an art form"--Peggy Pavelski).

220 CHANGING THE LAW, by Elvira Launt, n.d. (New Women and the Law Series.) 30 min. b/w. Douglas College.
Shows how the lay person can go about changing the laws (in Canada), how to lobby for changes you want to see made.

221 CHRISTIAN FEMINISM, by the Vancouver Status of Women Commission, 1976. 30 min. color. Douglas College.
Interview with two women who attended the Canadian Conference of Women in Religion in 1975. They talk about the concept of feminism in Christianity.

222 COMING OUT OF VIOLENCE, by Eggplant Media Productions, 1978. (No time or color information avail.) Eggplant Media Productions.

Most of the material was taken at a public hearing on the problem of battered women organized by the U.S. Commission on Civil Rights in Hartford, Conn. The battered women testify about the psychological and physical manifestations of battering. Also testimony is given by people working in Social Service Departments, courts, police departments, and hospitals. Also battered women are interviewed and shown in support groups and in shelters.

223 COMMUNAL LIVING--AN ALTERNATIVE, by Linda Vance, 1973. 30 min. Linda Vance.

The program asks people in urban and rural communes why they opted for communal living and what the effects this life style has on personal relationships, sex roles, children, and their ambition.

224 COMMUNITY PROPERTY by Elvira Launt, n.d. (New Women and the Law Series.) 30 min. b/w. Douglas College.

Outlines the history of community property, where the system is used and how it works in those areas. Includes a discussion on the pros and cons of the scheme. (Canada.)

225 COMMON-LAW MARRIAGE, by Elvira Launt, n.d. (New Women and the Law Series.) 30 min. b/w. Douglas College.

Deals with the differences between legal and common-law marriages. Covers the right of the common-law spouse and any children in regard to property, wills, income, tax, and support. (Canada.)

226 CONCERNS OF AMERICAN INDIAN WOMEN, by WNED-TV, 1977. 29 min. color. Public Television Library.

Dr. Connie Redbird Uri, a physician and member of the Choctaw Cherokee Tribe, and Maria Sanchez, Chief Judge of the Northern Cheyenne Tribe, discuss the problems of American Indian Women.

227 CONGRESSMAN JOHN BURTON: WOMEN IN CONGRESS, by House Recording Studio, 1975. 30 min. color, Barbara Boxer.

Discussion with Representative Pat Schroeder of Colorado, Representative Martha Keys of Kansas and Congressman John Burton of California on problems encountered by women in politics. The two women representatives tell some of the problems faced in Congress and steps they have taken to overcome them.

228 CONSCIOUSNESS RAISING, by Canadian Women, n.d. 30 min. b/w. Satellite Video Exchange Society.
The group discusses monogamy, clothing, divorce, and children's stories--a documentary of a consciousness-raising session.

229 CONTEMPORARY WOMEN POETS, by WNED-TV, 1976. 29 min. color. Public Television Library.
Poet Audrie Lord and poet/novelist Marge Piercy read and discuss their works and share their views on contemporary poetry.

230 A CONVERSATION WITH JEANNE MOREAU, PART 1 AND 2, by WNED-TV, 1976. 29 min. ea. color. Public Television Library.
Jeanne Moreau shares her view on men, women and directors. She talks about her career and the difficulties she has encountered reconciling her domestic and professional roles. She also comments on the lack of female parts in American films.

231 A CONVERSATION WITH LOTTE JACOBI, by WNED-TV, 1977. 29 min. color. Public Television Library.
Portrait photographer Lotte Jacobi discusses her life, politics, and photographs. Some of the subjects of her photography have been Eleanor Roosevelt, Robert Frost, Marc Chagall, Lotte Lenya, and Albert Einstein.

232 A CONVERSATION WITH ROBIN MORGAN, by WNED-TV, 1977. 29 min. color. Public Television Library.
Author and feminist Robin Morgan discusses her personal philosophy and assesses the progress of the women's movement. She describes how her roles as wife and mother have affected her politics, and how they have, in turn, been influenced by her activism.

233 A CONVERSATION WITH SIMONE DE BEAUVOIR, by WNED-TV, 1977. 60 min. color. Public Television Library.
Author and feminist Simone de Beauvoir discusses her work and philosophy. She talks about the abortion issue, which led her to take an active role in the women's movement. Following the interview, Gloria Steinem and Elizabeth Janeway discuss the impact de Beauvoir has had on the women's movement.

234 DANCE SOAP, by Marien Lewis, 1973. 54 min. b/w. Satellite Video Exchange Society.
The documentation of the preparation for a wedding.

235 DEL MARTIN AND PHYLLIS LYON, by Women in Focus, 1975. 30 min. color. Women in Focus.
　　The authors of Lesbian Woman discuss their book, lesbianism, motherhood, relationships and other topics.

236 DR. DOROTHY SMITH: AN INTERVIEW, by Women in Focus, 1975. 30 min. color. Women in Focus.
　　Dr. Dorothy E. Smith, University of British Columbia Sociologist, discusses how women have been excluded from forming the knowledge, ideas and beliefs of our society.

237 DR. EVA JESSYE: BLACK AMERICAN FOLK MUSIC, by Cheryl Stereff/Innerflex Media, 1977. 30 min. b/w. Innerflex Media.
　　Recollections of the first black woman to earn international distinction as a choral director. Original stills, music by the Eva Jessye choir.

238 DR. MORGENTALER SPEAKS, by Barb Steinman/Chris Gerrish-Woman Alive, 1974. 30 min. b/w. Video Inn.
　　Dr. Morgentaler talks about repealing existing abortion laws, the position of women wanting abortions, and his impending trials. Documentation of a speech at the University of British Columbia.

239 DR. PEPPER SCHWARTZ, by Women in Focus, 1975. 30 min. color. Women in Focus.
　　Dr. Schwartz talks about her recent research regarding bisexuality.

240 EXPERIMENT IN EQUALITY: THE WOMEN'S VOTE, by WTL Productions, 1972. 26 min. color. WTL Productions.
　　Examines the impact of women's suffrage on United States society.
　　Review: Booklist, March 1, 1977, p1031 ("Use of highly appropriate and interesting illustrations, rare film footage ... will be of interest to community groups, public libraries and educators"--Jane Braun).

241 FASHION AS SOCIAL CONTROL, by Women in Focus, 1975. 30 min. color. Women in Focus.
　　Deals with fashion as it has affected and continues to affect women. Slides, photographs, fashion plates, and models wearing authentic period costumes depict the changes in dress and the resulting effect upon women.

242 FEMALE HOMOSEXUALITY, by WNED-TV, 1974. 30 min. color. Public Television Library.

Discusses author Barbara Love's "coming out" as a lesbian and some of the problems faced by female homosexuals in today's world.

243 FEMINIST FOLK SONGS: BEWARE YOUNG LADIES, by Women in Focus, 1975. 30 min. color. Women in Focus.
Local Canadian folksinger Eileen Brown talks about the songs she sings and presents a wide range of her favorites, which include Beware Young Ladies and Cotton Mill Girls.

244 FEMINIST THEATRE, by Women in Focus, 1975. 30 min. color. Women in Focus.
Two Vancouver actresses, Svetlana Smith and Miriam Weinstein, discuss what it means to be a feminist in the world of theatre, the problems of being a woman and an artist, and the future of feminist theatre groups.

245 FERRON AT CO-OP RADIO, by Shawn Preus, 1976. 22 min. b/w. Satellite Video Exchange Society.
Several songs written and sung by Ferron at Co-op Radio in Vancouver in 1976,

246 FOR COLORED GIRLS WHO HAVE CONSIDERED SUICIDE, by Shameless Hussy Press, 1975. 32 min. color. Shameless Hussy Press.
Ntozake Shange is a San Francisco Bay Area poet. In this tape Shange reads her poetry to a dance accompaniment. A visual documentation of the poet's work.

247 GETTING MARRIED, by Elvira Launt, n.d. (New Women and The Law Series.) 30 min. b/w. Douglas College.
Includes a brief history of marriage, deals with topics such as age of consent, when marriages are invalid, marriage contracts, nationality, and credit. (Canada.)

248 GIVING BIRTH: FOUR PORTRAITS, by Julie Gustafson and John Reilly, 1976. 60 min. color. Video Studio Center, Global Village.
The tape shows four different births. The first one is the usual high-technology delivery. The next one is a home delivery by a physician; the third a hospital birth that turns into an emergency and the fourth is a midwife delivery in an innovative maternity center. Leading professional advocates of each of these approaches state their case.
Reviews: Popular Photography, February 1977 ("a most remarkable video tape, one that rescues the documentary from its current humdrum"--Leendert Drukker). New York Times, December 17, 1976 ("most valuable in suggesting alternatives within the birth experience"--John J. O'Connor). Los Angeles Times, December 17, 1976.

249 GLADYS, A QUEEN IN EXILE, by N. Bethune Levine, n.d. 35 min. b/w. Satellite Video Exchange Society.
A Montreal poverty area is seen through the eyes of a waitress from the Prince Arthur Cafe.

250 GREASE, by Sharon Lovett, 1976. 15 min. b/w. Video Inn.
A brief look at a women's garage with commentary on women and their work in this field.

251 GREAT ARTISTS, by Women in Focus, 1975. 30 min. color. Women in Focus.
Artist Theo L. Turner talks about female power concepts as found in ancient mythology. The works and background of artists in the period 1500-1800 are illustrated. Artists include Catharina Van Henessen, Sofonisba Anguissola, Lavinia Fontana, Artemisia Gentileschi, Judith Leyster, Maria Sibylla Merian, Rachel Ruysch, Rosalba Carriera, Angelica Kauffman, Elizabeth Vigee-Lebrun, Adelaide Labille-Guiard, and Constance Marie Charpentier.

252 HARD LABOUR, by Ross Gentleman and Barb Steinman, 1975. 23 min. b/w. Satellite Video Exchange Society.
It was to be a home birth, but 40 hours of labor leads to a hospital birth. The mother still believes in the benefits of home birth but warns that it is not always possible.

253 HIGH SCHOOL WOMEN, by the Vancouver Status of Women Commission. 1975. 30 min. color. Douglas College.
Three high-school women discuss the sexist problems they encounter in their schools. The areas of discussion range from sports, curriculum, teachers and textbooks to dating, clothes, and competition.

254 HOMEMADE TV: BEING A PARENT--BEING A CHILD, by Bonnie Klein, Joanne Giardini, Susan Goddard, 1975. 30 min. b/w. Portable Channel.
In the first part a father discusses his role as father and the changes that the women's movement has had on his feelings about fatherhood. The second part of the tape is a look at the world through the eyes of a child.

255 HOW TO START YOUR OWN BUSINESS, PART I, PART II, by WNED-TV, 1976. 29 min. (each part). Public Television Library.
Part I: Claudia Jessup and Genie Chipps, co-authors of The Women's Guide to Starting a Business, discuss the risks, procedures and rewards for women starting their own businesses. Part II: Ann Smith, owner of a

restaurant in Connecticut, and Ava Stern, publisher of a national newsletter for women business-owners, Artemis for Enterprising Women, recount their experiences in starting and operating businesses.

256 HUMOR BY WOMEN, by WNED-TV, 1976. 29 min. color. Public Television Library.
Writers Anne Beatts and Deanne Stillman tell about their book--the first book of women's humor. They explain the concept of the book, Titters.

257 IN MOURNING AND IN RAGE, by L.A. Women's Video Center, 1978. 30 min. L.A. Women's Video Center.
Documents a social art performance staged at City Hall in Los Angeles, mourning women victims of violence and sexual abuse. Includes a press conference and speak-out with women from organizations dealing with violence against women and members of the Los Angeles City Council.

258 INNER VISION/BEAH RICHARDS, by KCET-TV, 1975. 29 min. color. Public Television Library.
Actress-playwright-poet Richards reads from her book A Black Woman Speaks and Other Poems and talks about her life and her strong feelings about women's liberation.

259 INTERNATIONAL TRIBUNALS ON CRIMES AGAINST WOMEN, by WNED-TV, 1977. 29 min. color. Public Television Library.
The investigation of crimes against women by two international tribunals, the International Tribunal on Crimes Against Women, Brussels, and the New York Tribunal. The tribunals considered subjects ranging from forced motherhood to the workload of working women to medical crimes.

260 IT CAN BE DONE, Kartemquin/Haymarket Films, 1974. 30 min. b/w. Insight Exchange.
The Chicago Women's Graphics Collective gets together with Women of the United Farm Workers to design and make a silk screen poster for the United Farm Workers' boycott of nonunion lettuce and grapes.

261 IT'S NOT MY HEAD, IT'S MY BODY, by Reseau Video des Femmes, 1978. 50 min. b/w. Women in Focus.
About strippers--who they are, what becomes of them, how they live and how they perceive their work and society's view of their work. (Rental is limited by request of the producer to women only audiences.)

262 JOURNALISTS AT INTERNATIONAL WOMEN'S YEAR, by Martha Stuart Communications, 1975. 28 min. color. Martha Stuart Communications.

A panel discussion of women journalists from many countries all over the world who attended and covered the International Women's Year Conference in Mexico City in 1975. They discuss the highlights of the conference.
Reviews: New York Daily News, December 30, 1975 p52 ("While what these women have to say ... is significant, there is something even more significant.... Suddenly to see full-blown women with depth, who can combine achievement with femininity ... is like a dash of cold water in the face"). New York Amsterdam News, January 17, 1976, p16, Majority Report, January 10-24, 1976, p16.

263 KARATE AND SELF-DEFENSE, by Women in Focus, 1975. 30 min. color. Women in Focus.
The basic techniques and skills of self-defense are demonstrated; vulnerable points of the body and simple methods for parrying a variety of attacks and suggestions for dealing verbally and physically with aggression are illustrated.

264 KATE MILLET: LECTURE AT CLATSOP COMMUNITY COLLEGE, by Rebecca Rubens, 1977. 60 min. b/w. Rebecca Rubens.

265 KEEPING THE DOOR OPEN--ANN SCHAFER, by Kin Beaman and Lydia Kleiner, 1974. 20 min. color. Women and Work Video.
Focuses on the life of Ann Schafer, a labor negotiator, feminist and founding member of the Coalition of Labor Union Women, who has worked on the line at Kellogg's in Battle Creek, Michigan, for nearly thirty years.

266 KEY WOMEN AT INTERNATIONAL WOMEN'S YEAR, by Martha Stuart Communications, 1975. 28 min. color. Martha Stuart Communications.
Shows a discussion group composed of women delegates at the 1975 Mexico City Conference on Women's Rights. The delegates present the highlights of the Conference.
Reviews: Booklist, January 15, 1976, p56 ("camera and audio work are good"; "a number of interesting insights on the problems of third world women, ideological differences that stalled the I.W.Y. Conference, and various courses of action which women around the world should take to improve their circumstances"). New York Amsterdam News, January 17, 1976, p16. Majority Report, January 10-24, 1976, p6.

267 LEAVING FOR THE SEA, by Catherine Brunelle, 1978. 30 min. b/w. Women in Focus.
A dream-like video fiction, devised and played by women. (By request of the producers, rental is limited to women-only audiences.)

268 LEGISLATIVE REPORT, by WNED-TV, 1976. 29 min. color. Public Television Library.
Carol Burris, president of the Women's Lobby, Inc., discusses current proposed legislation that would benefit women. Topics discussed are child-care credit, various national health care plans. the Humphrey-Hawkins Bill, and displaced homemakers' legislation.

269 LEGISLATIVE REPORT UPDATE, by WNED-TV, 1977. 29 min. color. Public Television Library.
Washington lobbyists Carol Burris and Susan Tenenbaum describe the role of the lobbyist and the progress of current legislation affecting women.

270 LESBIAN MOTHERS AND CHILD CUSTODY, PART 1 AND 2, by WNED-TV, 1977. 29 min. ea. color. Public Television Library.
Part 1: Attorneys Barbara Handschu and Margot Hagman discuss the struggle of lesbian mothers to retain custody of their children. Part 2: Two lesbian women describe their efforts to reclaim custody of one of the women's son who has been placed under his father's guardianship as the result of a jury trial at which the lesbianism of the mother was the central issue.

271 LIBERATION MEDIA, by Lyn Wright, 1972. 27 min. b/w. Women's Involvement Program, c/o Lyn Wright.
A feminist history of Canada.

272 LIKE THE TREES, by Kathleen Shannon, 1973. 15 min. b/w. Video Inn.
A native American mother, abandoned by her husband, tells of her struggle to support herself.

273 LOIS GOULD ON WOMEN WRITERS, by WNED-TV, 1977. 29 min. color. Public Television Library.
Novelist and journalist Lois Gould discusses women as writers--traditional assumptions about women writers and how that affects the literature and her feelings about the responsibility of the woman author to other women.

274 LOOKING FOR A JOB? by Women in Focus, 1975. 30 min. color. Women in Focus.
Four women talk about their experiences and problems in looking for and finding a job.

275 LOS ANGELES VIDEOLETTERS, by Los Angeles Feminist Video Outlet, 1975. 30 min. b/w. Los Angeles Feminist Video Outlet.
Various topics explored are: striking workers, the case of Yvonne Wanrow, diet programs. Footage of a demonstration against a diet program business, a women's benefit concert are shown.

276 LOS ANGELES WOMEN'S COMMUNICATIONS COLLECTIVE NEWS AND ANALYSIS SHORTS, 1978, by Los Angeles Women's Communications Collective, 1978. 60 min. b/w. Los Angeles Women's Communications Collective.
The programs are (1) protest against forced sterilization, (2) Free Emma Viser, (3) Hiroshima-Nagasaki Memorial and protest, (4) Women's surface day celebration, (5) Labor Day--United Farm workers, (6) Venice Canal Festival, (7) L.A. women's strike day--women in transition, (8) women's alcoholics program, (9) Free Olga Talamate, (10) Senate Bill # 1 information.

277 LOSING: A CONVERSATION WITH THE PARENTS, by Martha Rosler, 1977. 20 min. color. Women in Focus.
A young couple address an unseen questioner on the issues of the comfortable life and liberal sentiments and the implications for political action and theory.

278 MAD ABOUT THE CRAZY LADY, by Monica Holden Lawrence, n.d. 44 min. color. Satellite Video Exchange Society.
Monica Lawrence's poetry examines the lesbian world, male hierarchies imposed on them, and society's reactions to lesbianism.

279 MAINSTREAM, by KSPS-TV, 1976. 28 min. color. Public Television Library.
Filmed on the Coeur d'Alene Reservation in Idaho and in Spokane, the film is the story of a young Coeur d'Alene Indian woman's discovery of her ties to her family, land, and tribe.

280 MARGARET ATWOOD: AN INTERVIEW, by Women in Focus, 1975. 30 min. color. Women in Focus.
Margaret Atwood talks about her early aspirations to be a writer, her books, Canadian Nationalism and various other topics.

281 MARGARET MEAD: AN INTERVIEW, by Women in Focus, 1975. 30 min. color. Women in Focus.
World-famous anthropologist and author Margaret Mead talks about women in her own family and their influence upon her life, her work, and her experiences of being both a professional and family woman.

282 MARIE-CLAIRE BLAIS: AN INTERVIEW, by Women in Focus, 1975. 30 min color. Women in Focus.
Well-known French-Canadian author of <u>A Season in the Life of Emmanuel</u>, <u>Mad Shadows</u>, <u>The Manuscripts of Pauline Archange</u>, etc. talks about herself and her writing.

283 MASCULINE, FEMININE AND ANDROGYNY, by WNED-TV, 1977. 29 min. color. Public Television Library.
Psychologist Joan Bean talks about the meaning of an androgynous personality and its significance in the women's movement. The benefits of broadening concepts previously defined as masculine and feminine are discussed.

284 MATRIMONIAL PROPERTY, by Elvira Launt, n.d. (New Women and The Law Series.) 30 min. b/w. Douglas College.
Deals with topics such as bank accounts, family home, joint tenancy, pledging credit, and inheritance. (Canada.)

285 MEDIA IMAGES OF WOMEN, by the Vancouver Status of Women Commission, 1975. 30 min. b/w. Douglas College.
Two women talk about their active involvement in fighting sex discrimination in advertising. They give practical information on what a person or group can do to combat sexist advertising.

286 MEN IN THE WOMEN'S MOVEMENT, by the Vancouver Status of Women Commission, 1975. 30 min. b/w. Douglas College.
Interview with three married men whose wives' experiences brought them into sympathy with the women's movement. Gives the perspective of how men view the movement and its meaning to their lives.

287 MEN'S LIBERATION, by the Vancouver Status of Women Commission, 1976. 30 min. color. Douglas College.
Interview with a man involved with a men's group who talks about men's liberation. Examines the emerging awareness in men of their own lives and expectations, what men want to be liberated from, and the connection between men's liberation and feminism.

288 MOTHERS ARE WORKING PEOPLE, by N.F.B., 1973. 6 min. Satellite Video Exchange Society.
One woman talks about her problems as a working mother. She expresses the need for better day care and the need for day care organized to fit working people's schedules.

289 MOTHERS AS ARTISTS, by Shameless Hussy Press, n.d. 30 min. color. Shameless Hussy Press,
Several women, who have managed to combine their personal and professional lives successfully, recall the adjustments necessary for them to do so. The women discuss their work as artists and the difficulties they faced in establishing their careers.

290 MRS. MARY NORTON: SOCIALIST SUFFRAGETTE, by Women in Focus, 1975. 30 min. color. Women in Focus.
Mary Norton, Vancouver suffragist, reminisces about the Canadian women's struggle for the vote, the controversial issues, including temperance, and the women who worked to obtain suffrage.

291 NATIONAL LESBIAN CONFERENCE, 1973, by Vulva Video, 1973. 25 min. b/w. Vulva Video.
General overview of the conference. Discussions of some of the issues (roles, raising children).

292 NEW ROLES FOR WOMEN IN SPORTS, by WNED-TV, 1977. 29 min. color. Public Television Library.
A discussion about the changing roles of women in athletics. The traditional attitudes of women toward sports and the historical conditions responsible for them are discussed.

293 NEW SEXUALITY CONFERENCE, by Robin Schwartz, 1974. 50 min. b/w. Robin Schwartz.
Tape cross-cuts scenes of speakers at the conference with informal discussion groups. Documents the 1973 Sexuality Conference of NOW.

294 NORTHERN IRISH PEOPLE'S PEACE MOVEMENT, PART 1 AND 2, by WNED-TV, 1977. 29 min. (each part). color. Public Television Library.
Betty Williams and Mairead Corrigan, leaders of the women's peace movement in Northern Ireland, discuss politics, their goals for peace, and the status of new Irish womanhood.

295 THE NORTHERN IRISH QUESTION: ANOTHER VIEW, by WNED-TV, 1977. 29 min. color. Public Television Library.
Patricia Davidson, press officer for the Ulster Provisional Sinn Fein, and Mary McNicholl, secretary of the United Brooklyn Irish, discuss the Irish Republican Movement's potential plans for peace and the part Irish women are playing in the Irish conflict.

296 OUR BODIES, OUR SELVES, REEL FEELINGS, by Reel Feelings, 1973. 24 min. b/w. Reel Feelings.
Details information on Vancouver Health Collective, gynecological information about self-examination, what to expect from your doctor, birth control methods, birth and general health.

297 O'WOMEN SERIES: WOMEN AND THE LAW, by Consumnes River College, 1975. 30 min. each. color. Consumnes River College.

Examines the current status of federal and California legislation affecting the rights of women. Part I, Federal Legislation, Part II, California Legislation.
Review: California Video Resource Project Patch Panel, November/December 1976, p21 ("interesting and informative"; "would provide a good basis for discussion on any number of topics relating to women's rights or the women's movement"--Carol Brown).

298 THE PARIS COMMUNE, 1871, by Women in Focus, 1975. 30 min. color. Women in Focus.
The women's contribution to the workers of the 1871 revolution, their proposals to the Commune's Assembly on topics such as education, childcare, working conditions, and women's rights, and the courageous women involved.

299 THE PEOPLE VS. INEZ GARCIA, by KQED-TV, 1977. 88 min. color. Public Television Library.
A dramatization of the rape and murder trial of Inez Garcia. It is based on the actual court transcription of the 1974 trial in Monterey, California. The drama raises important questions about the American criminal system and the right of a woman to defend herself in the context of an alleged rape.

300 PEOPLE'S PLAYGROUP, by Venice Women's Film Collective, 1972. 17 min. b/w. Satellite Video Exchange Society.
A member-operated day care center explains itself in action.

301 POLICEWOMEN, by the Vancouver Status of Women Commission, 1976. 30 min. color. Douglas College.
Three policewomen talk about what it is like to be a woman in law enforcement. They talk about their personal history, experiences in training, what the job entails, and how they have dealt with the attitudes of their coworkers and the public.

302 POLITICS OF INTIMACY, by Julie Gustafson, 1974. 43 min. Global Village, Video Study Center.
Ten women, ranging in age from 15 to 74, talk about their sexuality. The interviews are arranged by topic and are intercut throughout by an interview with Dr. Mary Jane Sherfey, author of the Nature and Evolution of Female Sexuality.

303 PORTRAIT OF THREE CHINESE-AMERICAN WOMEN, by the Asian-American Theatre Workshop, n.d. 28 min. b/w. Asian-American Theatre Workshop.
Three Chinese actresses from A.C.T. perform interesting monologues. Next, the author and director of

Chicken Coop Chinaman talks with a student and a teacher from A.C.T.

304 PROFILES OF WOMEN, by June Boe, 1972. 15 min. b/w. June Boe.
Women talk about commercial beauty and natural beauty as their profiles are being displayed on the monitor. Also there is an interview with Evelyn Roth and an excerpt from her "Wearables Performance" at the Vancouver Art Gallery.

305 RAPE, by Women Alive, 1974. 29 min. b/w. Women Alive, Cable 10.
Studio interviews with two women: one from Rape Relief, a Vancouver organization devoted to helping victims recover from the shock of the crime, and another with B.C. Status of Women.

306 RAPE IS A SOCIAL DISEASE, by Women in Focus, 1975. 30 min. color. Women in Focus.
The tape begins with a look at the image of women and rape as presented in classical art and modern-day advertising. Some of the most common myths surrounding rape are pointed out using amusing enactments and skits.

307 RAPE RELIEF, by the Vancouver Status of Women Commission, 1975. 30 min. b/w Women in Focus.
Information on all aspects of rape. Covers police procedure in dealing with rape, what the criminal code says about rape, and the myths and educational needs concerning rape.

308 RAPE: THE REALITY, by Elaine Velasquez, 1975. 40 min. b/w. Elaine Velasquez.
A documentary on rape, exploring women's experiences, society's attitudes and services available in Portland aiding the rape victim.

309 RECORD COMPANIES DRAG THEIR FEET, by L.A. Women's Video Center, 1978. 15 min. L.A. Women's Video Center.
Documents a social art performance directed at record companies protesting the use of violent images of women to promote their products.

310 RENAISSANCE, by Irene Halikas, n.d. 15 min. b/w. Irene Halikas.
Woman re-experiences images of her life, her children, her marriage, romance and loneliness.

311 RULE OF THUMB, by Peg Campbell, 1977. 30 min. Peg Campbell.

A documentary about battered wives. One woman's story is intercut with information from a counselor at Transition House in Vancouver.

312 RUTHIE GORTON: FOLK SINGER, by Women in Focus, 1975. 30 min. color. Women in Focus.

Feminist folksinger Gorton from Los Angeles sings a selection of her own and others' folksongs, including Private Property and Crazy Ruthie; she talks about how the songs reflect her experiences and feelings as a woman and a singer.

313 SALOME, by Robert Mickelson, 1974. 17 min. b/w. Robert Mickelson.

Myth, woman, and video are celebrated in an adaptation of Oscar Wilde's play.

314 SELF-HELP CLINIC, by Mo Simpson and Jan Cornflower, 1973. 20 min. b/w. Douglas College.

Records a woman's first visit to the clinic of the Vancouver Women's Health Collective. She learns of the origin and ideology of the clinic.

315 SELF-HELP HEALTH WITH JOAN MILLER, by Red River Community College, 1975. 55 min. b/w. Satellite Video Exchange Society.

A discussion between Joan Miller and several women on women's health problems and experiences. Includes breast and cervical self-examinations.

316 SEPARATION AND DIVORCE, by Elvira Launt, n.d. (New Women and The Law Series.) 30 min. b/w. Douglas College.

Examines aspects of separation and divorce such as separation agreements, court orders for separation, grounds for divorce and briefly outlines the procedure for obtaining a divorce. (Canada.)

317 SEXISM IN THE SCHOOLS, by Women in Focus, 1975. 30 min. color. Women in Focus.

Linda Shuto, British Columbia Teachers' Federation, Status of Women Task Force, states the evidence of sexism in the school system and discusses the problem using pertinent statistics.

318 SHOPPING BAG LADIES, by Vediamo Productions, 1978. 45 min. b/w. Vediamo Productions.

Shopping Bag Ladies are homeless women who live on the streets. This videotape moves with them through New York City as they pick for food in the garbage, make clothes out of rags, sleep outside in all weather. The women interviewed tell about their lives.

319 SHOULDER TO SHOULDER, by The BBC, 1975. 4 tapes (one hour each), b/w. Douglas College.
Parts 3, 4, 5, 6 of the BBC series. The story of the suffragettes is portrayed. Each tape is fully introduced and complete within itself.

320 A SIGN OF AFFECTION?, by Peg Campbell and Robert Boyd, n.d. 25 min. b/w. Peg Campbell.
A documentary about battered wives. A survey of attitudes and opinions from women who have been battered and those that are supposedly there to help them--i.e., social workers, doctors, police, a priest...

321 SISTER SOUNDS AND STEPPING OUT, by Suzanne C. Fox, 1975. 30 min. color. b/w. Suzanne C. Fox.
Introduces the members of two feminist performing arts collectives, Sister Sounds and Stepping Out, through actual performances and interviews.
Review: California Video Resource Project Patch Panel, January/February 1976, p18 ("A very effective record of how some political philosophies are reached, and an entertaining piece on the performing arts"--Peggy Pavelski).

322 SOME VOICES, SOME VISIONS, by Women Video Tape Artists, n.d. 6 tapes (one hour each) color. University of South Florida.
(1) Art and Life: Hermine Freed. (2) Time and Place: Shiziko Kubuta. (3) A New Beginning: Steina Vaksykja. (4) Women Talking About Themselves: Julie Gustafson. (5) Lesbians Organized for Video Experience: Love. (6) About Environments: Susan Milano.

323 SOMETIMES IT'S AWFUL HARD--FIVE WORKING WOMEN, by Kin Beaman and Lydia Kleiner, n.d. 30 min. color. Women and Work Video.
Highlights the work and home lives of five women: a homemaker and volunteer, a lawyer, a retired household worker, an ambulance attendant and a grocery store checker. Examines important issues confronting working women.

324 SOUR GRAPES: OUR PATRIARCHAL HERITAGE, by Women's Involvement Program. 1972. 16 min. b/w. Women's Involvement Program, c/o Lynn Wright.
A collage of dramatic readings by male actors from writings about women, with feminist rebuttal in poetry.

325 STONE SYMPOSIUM. by Women in Focus, 1975. 30 min. color. Women in Focus.
Three internationally renowned sculptors, Anna-Marie Kubach-Wilmsen (Germany), Olga Jancic (Yugoslavia),

and Joan Gambioli (Canada), discuss their art and their lives as artists and women.

326 SUGAR AND SPIKES, by Carol Cole, Rosemay Wiemer, and Tom Klinkostein, 1975. 30 min. color. b/w. Insight Exchange Incorporated.
Sheds light on controversial issues surrounding women in sports. Mixes live action sports with interviews with little league players, coaches, sports broadcasters, and professional woman athletes.

327 SUPERDYKE MEETS MADAM X, by May Almy and Barbara Hammer, 1975. 20 min. b/w. May Almy and Barbara Hammer.
A video diary of two gay women who are exploring their individual feelings and their intense personal relationship with each other.
Review: California Video Resource Project Patch Panel, July/August 1976, p17 ("bold and effective use of the medium"--Peggy Pavelski).

328 SYLVA GELBER: AN INTERVIEW, by Women in Focus, 1975. 30 min. color. Women in Focus.
The director of the Women's Bureau of Labor in Canada discusses many aspects of women's position within the labor force, the status of women in other countries, International Women's Year, and the statistical and informational publication which the Women's Bureau produces.

329 TAKE HER SHE'S MAD, by Marta Segovia Ashley (Femedia). 20 min. b/w. Marta Segovia Ashley (Femedia).
Dramatic portrayal of a 38-year-old woman in a psychiatric hospital.

330 THIRTEEN, by Jan Zimmerman, 1973. 19 min. b/w. Jan Zimmerman.
Thirteen-year-old girls talk about clothes, school, shopping, boys, etc. A portrait of adolescence.

331 TI-GRACE ATKINSON: RADICAL ACTIVIST/POLITICAL THEORIST, by Women in Focus, 1977. 28 min. color. Women in Focus.
An interview with Ti-Grace Atkinson in which she discusses the historical perspective of her feminism, examines the terms "feminist" and "class," and talks about the parts played in the women's movement by Socialist Feminism.

332 TOMORROW'S LEADERS, by Women in Focus, 1975. 30 min. color. Women in Focus.
A drama group from Kensington High School in Burnaby, British Columbia, act in a series of dramatizations of their own creation. Their work amusingly depicts female

and male role stereotyping through the use of role-reversal technique.

333 THE TWO EARNER FAMILY, by WNED-TV, 1976. 29 min. color. Public Television Library.
Writer Susan Edmiston and economist Dr. Carolyn Shaw Bell examine the sociological and economic implications of women entering the work force in increasing numbers.

334 VERBAL SELF-DEFENSE, by the Vancouver Status of Women Commission, 1976. 30 min. color. Douglas College.
On the art of verbal self-defense. Women need to know how to handle verbal put-down and this program gives lots of ideas on what to say to things like, "Why aren't you married yet?"

335 VIRGINIA, by Alan Bloom, 1974. 20 min. b/w. Alan Bloom.
Portrait of a 68-year-old woman; an individual portrait in the context of a repressive society.
Review: California Video Resource Project Patch Panel, January/February 1976, p16 ("a highly acclaimed winner at the 1975 San Francisco Art Festival's Mobius Video Pavilion"--Peggy Pavelski).

336 VITAL STATISTICS OF A CITIZEN, SIMPLY OBTAINED, by Martha Rosler, 1977. Women in Focus.
A nondocumentary examination of the objectification of women and others in modern society.

337 WELL KEPT SECRETS REVEALED, by Insight Exchange Incorporated, 1975. 60 min. b/w. Insight Exchange Incorporated.
Documentary showing the reaction of seven women, all over fifty, to social change.
Review: California Video Resource Project Patch Panel, July/August 1975, p21 ("The tape has value, not only in a feminist program, but in programs on senior citizens in general, as it offers a fresh insight into their reactions to social change"--Peggy Pavelski).

338 WHAT WILL I BE, by Women in Focus, n.d. 30 min. color. Women in Focus.
The tape starts with a short historical look at women's position in education. Two leading authorities on sexism in the school system relate their opinions on the problems of sexism and give some solutions. The tape ends with Grade Six students critically discussing sex role stereotyping.

339 WHEN YOU HAVE CHILDREN, by Elvira Launt, n.d. (New Women and The Law Series.) 30 min. color. Douglas College.

Deals with legal responsibilities toward your children, your children and the law, and children's rights. (Canada.)

340 WHO NEEDS DAYCARE?, by Audrey Bryant, 1974. 25 min. color. Audrey Bryant.
Interviews show the importance of daycare for children and their families.

341 WIFE BEATING, by NBC, 1976. 27 min. color. Films Incorporated.
One of the most common forms of violence in the country, wife beating, is coming out into the open. The film examines the psychology of wife beating, the emotional as well as physical repercussions on women and their children and possible remedies to a widespread social problem.

342 WOMAN SERIES: THE EQUAL RIGHTS AMENDMENT, by WNED-TV, 1974. 29 min. color. Public Television Library.
Part I. Ann Scott, head of the Washington, D.C., office of NOW and Karen De Crow, lawyer and author, discuss the issues raised by the ERA, with special emphasis on its expected economic impact. Part II. Presents the views of two opponents to the ERA.
Review: California Video Resource Project Patch Panel, July/August 1976, p16 ("generated one of the liveliest and best audience discussions of the year"--Peggy Pavelski).

343 WOMEN AND HEART ATTACKS, PART 1 AND 2, by WNED-TV, 1977. 29 min. (each part) color. Public Television Library.
Doctors Nanette Wenger and Harriet Dustan discuss women and heart attacks. Subjects examined include the effects of birth control pills, physical activity, diet, smoking, alcohol, sex, and health education.

344 WOMEN AND SUCCESS, by WNED-TV, 1977. 29 min. color. Public Television Library.
Sociologist Adeline Levine talks about women and the idea of success. She examines the origin of the idea that women are afraid of success, how women are taught to regard work and what women can do to stimulate their own success.

345 WOMEN AND TAXES, by WNED-TV, 1977. 29 min. color. Public Television Library.
Martha Yates, author of the book Coping: A Survival Manual for Woman Alone, discusses recent changes in federal tax laws that have made tax credits available for child-care expenses.

346 WOMEN AND THE ARTS, by Reel Feelings, 1973. 30 min. b/w. Douglas College.
Six women artists, each involved with a different medium (dance, poetry, sculpture, theatre), are recorded at work. Several of the women discuss their committment to their work and how it has been shaped or affected by marriage, children, etc.

347 WOMEN AND THE LAW: AN INTRODUCTION, by WTL Productions, 1976. 28 min. color. WTL Productions.
Examines the impact of the ERA on existing laws and social attitudes, treatment of female offenders, marriage and divorce laws.
Review: <u>Booklist</u>, December 1, 1976, p558 ("Especially effective from a technical standpoint, the series ... is valuable for its content on an important topic"--Jane Braun).

348 WOMEN ARTISTS, by Mo Simpson, n.d. 30 min. b/w. Mo Simpson.
Jazz dancers, followed by two poets and two singers.

349 WOMEN AT WORK: EMPLOYMENT DISCRIMINATION, by Seattle Feminist Video, 1978. 30 min. b/w. Women in Focus.
Discusses employment discrimination against women in both traditional and nontraditional jobs. One section of the video was filmed at the International Women's Year Convention, 1977, and another section contains interviews with personnel working in the Seattle office of Women's Rights and the Human Rights Department.

350 WOMEN COMPOSERS, by Women in Focus, 1975. 30 min. color. Women in Focus.
A presentation of classical composers from the middle ages to modern times. Included are Francesca Caccini, Maria Therea Von Paradis, Fanny Mendelssohn, Clara Wieck Schumann, Germaine Tailleferre, Lili Boulanger, and modern composers Sonia Eckhardt-Grammate, Barbara Pentland, Victoria Bond, and Jean Coulthard. Examples of their work are included.

351 WOMEN IN ART: PAST AND PRESENT, by Alan Garfield, n.d. 5 tapes (30 min. ea.) Dr. Alan Garfield.
Each videotape examines the relationship between women artists and their particular historic and artistic time. Program 1 is a discussion of the creative process and also examines the spirituality in the work of Sabina von Steinbock and the Italian Renaissance engravings of Diana Ghisi. Program 2 discusses the Renaissance women artists of the

Women's Nonprint Media   54

16th century. Program 3 examines the art of Italy in the 16th and 17th centuries. Artists and works shown are Plautilla Nelli, Marietta Robusti, and Artemisia Gentileschi. Program 4 covers the Baroque period in the Netherlands, Italy, and France, 19th-century realism in America and France, 20th-century American Modernism. Some of the artists included are: Judith Leyster, Rosalba Carriera, Henrietta Johnson, Elizabeth Vigee-Lebrun, Rosa Bonheur, Isabel Bishop, and May Stevens. Program 5 is a conversation with four contemporary artists, Nancy Osborne, Pamela Opliger, Betty Jane Bramlett, and Sara Oliphant.

352 WOMEN IN MEDIA: AN INTERVIEW WITH ELAINE VELASQUEZ, by Rebecca Rubens. n.d. 20 min. color. Rebecca Reubens.
   Elaine Velasquez is the former director of Video Access in Portland, Oregon, and a video artist.

353 WOMEN IN NEWSPAPER MANAGEMENT, 1979. 7 videotapes. Women in Newspaper Management.
   Series of seven tapes discussing the current status of women in newspaper management, as well as the psychological, social, legal, and practical problems faced by women in the field.

354 WOMEN IN THE ARTS, by Reel Feelings, 1973. 21 min. b/w. Reel Feelings.
   The tape covers some of the work of Vancouver's women artists.

355 WOMEN IN THE FAMILY, by Ann Sutherland, 1973. 30 min. b/w. Women's Center, YWCA.
   With interpretations from a psychologist, women talk about power in husband-wife relationships.

356 WOMEN OF ERIN, by Catherine F. Hatch, 1975. 25 min. b/w. Caroline F. Hatch.
   Shows the conflict in Northern Ireland from the viewpoint of Irish Catholic women there.
   Review: <u>California Video Resource Project Patch Panel</u>, January/February 1976, p17 ("The changing role of Irish women due to the struggle with their subsequent questioning of old values and customs, is sharply defined in this dramatic tape"--Peggy Pavelski).

357 WOMEN OF THE WORLD, by Gail Swanson, 1975. 60 min. b/w. Gail Swanson.
   Describes three California women educators' firsthand experiences at, and reactions to, the World Conference of Women in Mexico City, 1975, where for the first time in history women from 133 nations met to discuss the problems unique to women.

358 WOMEN RALLY FOR ACTION, by Women in Focus, n.d. 30 min. color. Women in Focus.
This tape is a documentary of the Vancouver March 8 and Victoria March 22 "Women Rally for Action." Highlights from songs, speeches, lobbying reports and the general interaction that took place on this historic occasion are shown.

359 WOMEN SCULPTORS, by Leigh Deering and Mary Gillies, 1975. 30 min. b/w. Douglas College.
During July and August of 1975, the Vancouver School of Art hosted an international Stone Sculpture Symposium. The tape is about three women from Canada, Yugoslavia, and Germany who participated in the symposium.

360 WOMEN--THE NATIVE EXPERIENCE, by Gail Valaskakis, 1973. 30 min. b/w. Canadian Women TV Series.
The program examines the unique problems experienced by native American women in Canada and what is being done about them. Alternatives such as organizing, sharing common problems, relating to the traditional past, and integrated families are discussed.

361 WOMEN WITHIN TWO CULTURES, by Women in Focus, 1975. 30 min. color. Women in Focus.
This tape looks at the situation of the British Columbian West Indian women and the early white pioneer women. The presentation includes slides of native women within their own culture and how the coming of the white settlers disrupted their life.

362 WOMEN'S ASTROLOGY, by WNED-TV, 1977. 29 min. color. Public Television Library.
Tiffany Holmes, author of Women's Astrology: Your Astrological Guide to a Future Worth Having, is a professional astrologer. She discusses the negativism she finds in the traditional interpretation of astrology for women.

363 WOMEN'S CLINIC, by Mo Simpson, n.d. 15 min. b/w. Mo Simpson.
Describes how a women's clinic in Vancouver is working. People who work in the clinic talk about their work and the clinic.

364 WOMEN'S EDIT, by Optic Nerve, 1972. 6 min. b/w. Optic Nerve.
A visual exploration of the image of women, with particular emphasis on mannequins.

365 WOMEN'S LIB FROM SARAH, by Leni Goldberg, 1972. 18 min. b/w. Leni Goldberg.
In song and standup comedy, the male-female relationship is examined.

366 WOMEN'S POLITICAL DANCE, by Elaine Velasquez, 1975. 28 min. b/w. Elaine Velasquez.
The dances and songs are by and for women, celebrating the victory of Vietnam, healing, and the militant resistance of all women.

367 WOMEN'S STUDIES, by Women in Focus, 1975. 30 min. color. Women in Focus.
Dr. Meredith Kimball, women's studies teacher, University of British Columbia, and two of her students discuss what it means to take a women's studies course for academic credit, the problems of teaching and studying such a topic, and the kinds of changes it makes in the students and teachers.

368 THE WOMEN'S SUFFRAGE MOVEMENT IN CANADA, by Women in Focus, n.d. 30 min. color. Women in Focus.
Examines the women's suffrage movement, the women who were active at this time and some of the most controversial issues: temperance, motherhood and its obligations, and the vote.

369 WORKING CLASS WOMEN, by WNED-TV, 1977. 29 min. color. Public Television Library.
Nancy Seifer, director of the Center on Women and American Diversity, and Mary Sansone, director of the Congress of Italian American Organizations, examine the role of the working woman.

370 YVONNE WANROW, by Daryl Lacey, 1978. 28 min. b/w. Video Inn.
Documentation of a talk given by Yvonne Wanrow. She outlines the events leading up to her conviction on murder charges and her struggles to stay out of jail and to change the legal system that wants her imprisoned.

FILMSTRIPS

371 THE AMERICAN WOMAN: A SOCIAL CHRONICLE, by Teaching Resources Films, 1976. 6 filmstrips (78-93 fr.) color. (with phonorecords or cassettes) Teaching Resources Films.
 The filmstrips are entitled: (1) Puritans and Patriots, (2) Mill Girls, Intellectuals and the Southern Myth, (3) Pioneer Women and Belles of the Wild West, (4) The Suffragist, the Working Woman and the Flapper, (5) Breadlines, Assembly Lines and Togetherness, (6) Liberation Now.

372 AMERICAN WOMAN: NEW OPPORTUNITIES, by Chrome Yellow Films, 1976. 2 filmstrips. color. (with phonorecords or cassettes) Chrome Yellow Films.
 A view of the life, careers and relationships of the American woman today.
 Review: Booklist, May 15, 1976, p1352 ("A broad panorama of women's opportunities in the past and today, this filmstrip set utilizes each element to its fullest potential to incisively convey its message"--Beth Ames).

373 AND AIN'T I A WOMAN? by AIDS Audiovisual Instruction Devices, 1975. 6 filmstrips (13 min. each) color. (with phonorecord or cassettes) Schloat Productions.
 The filmstrips are entitled: (1) Early Signs, (2) The Feminist Fifties, (3) Hearthside, (4) Outside, (5) Society and Attitudes, (6) Toward a New Consciousness. Traces the progress of women through history. Features quotes from writings of women on the struggle for women's rights.

374 BEYOND ROLES, by Clifford Janoff, 1975. 1 filmstrip (81 fr.) color. (with phonorecord or cassette) BFA Educational Media.
 Discusses traditional masculine and feminine roles and shows how these roles are changing.

375 Brontë, Emily. WUTHERING HEIGHTS, by the Women's Audio Exchange, n.d. 2 filmstrips (2 cassettes). color. Women's Audio Exchange.

A dramatization of the famous novel.

376 THE CHANGING ROLE OF WOMEN. Associated Press Report, n.d. 2 filmstrips (2 cassettes or phonorecords) color. Prentice-Hall Media.
   Leading feminists discuss the historic struggle of women and the freedom, equality of opportunity, and self-identity of the modern woman. The impact of modern women on the world of today and the future is also examined.

377 FAMOUS WOMEN OF THE WEST, by Multi-Media Productions, 1974. 1 filmstrip (46 fr., 13 min.) color. (phonorecord) Multi-Media Productions.
   Reviews the contribution women of the West made to America in the 19th century. Discusses women as guides, entertainers, teachers, political activists, and unusual characters.
   Review: Previews, October 1975, p42 ("Female missionaries, pioneers, Indian guide, army wives and daughter ... are briefly glossed over in this program ... the filmstrip is impossible, the photographs and tin-types are passable but the drawings are inexcusable"--Mary Jean Weir).

378 LES FEMMES CÉLÉBRÉ DE L'HISTOIRE DE FRANCE (the Famous Women Who Made French History), by Audio Lingual Educational Press, 1976. 10 filmstrips (20 fr. each) (with cassettes) Audio Lingual Educational Press.
   Uses photographs, interviews, and narration to show the role of women in French history.

379 FOUR AMERICAN WOMEN ARTISTS, by Educational Dimensions Group, 1975. 2 filmstrips (78-91 fr., 17-21 min. each) (with cassettes) Educational Dimensions Group
   Discusses the work of two American painters, Georgia O'Keeffe and Helen Frankenthaler, and two American sculptors, Louise Nevelson and Marisol Escobar.
   Review: Previews, April 1976, p26 ("A female narrator with a most pleasant voice, an excellent script, and high quality photography make this set outstanding" --Mary Jean Weir).

380 HATSHEPSUT: THE FIRST WOMAN OF HISTORY, by Multi Media Productions, 1975. 2 filmstrips (116 fr., 35 min. each) (with phonorecord or cassettes) Multi Media Productions.
   Presents the story of Hatshepsut as Pharaoh of Egypt.

Review: Previews, May 1976, p45 ("Women's rights would be better advanced by more even treatment"--Pamela K. Kramer).

381 JOBS AND GENDER, Guidance Associates, n.d. 2 filmstrips (2 cassettes or phonorecords) color. Guidance Associates.
Examines sex-role stereotypes and job choices. Interviews with a female carpenter, a male registered nurse, a woman newspaper reporter, and two men who work in early childhood education present adults who have broken through the sexual barriers.

382 MALE AND FEMALE: HOW AWARE ARE YOU?, by Globe Filmstrips, 1975. 1 filmstrip (56 fr.) color. (with phonorecord or cassette) Coronet Instructional Media.
Provides a self-test for examining sexist attitudes and actions and discussing future life style options.
Review: Previews, November 1976, p32 ("A logically organized, competently presented series which presents a definite viewpoint while encouraging discussion and independent thought on essential issues"--Anitra Gordon).

383 MALE AND FEMALE ROLES: EMERGING DISSATISFACTIONS, by Globe Filmstrips, 1975. 1 filmstrip (67 fr.) color. (with phonorecord or cassette) Coronet Instructional Media.
Documents some of the major objections to stereotyped sex roles and raises the question as to whether there are better solutions.

384 MALE AND FEMALE ROLES: HOW STEREOTYPES EVOLVED, by Globe Filmstrips, 1975. 1 filmstrip (55 fr.) color. (with phonorecord or cassette) Coronet Instructional Media.
Explores some theories of how sex-role stereotypes may have developed through history.

385 MALE AND FEMALE ROLES: HOW THEY ARE LEARNED, by Globe Filmstrips, 1975. 1 filmstrip (63 fr.) color. (with phonorecord or cassettes) Coronet Instructional Media.
Examines ways American society directs males and females into two separate sex roles from birth.

386 MALE AND FEMALE ROLES: NEW PERSPECTIVES, by Globe Filmstrips, 1975. 1 filmstrip (61 fr.) color. (with phonorecord or cassette) Coronet Instructional Media.
Considers alternative sex roles available to men and women and the need for flexibility.

Women's Nonprint Media   60

387 MALE AND FEMALE ROLES: THE STEREOTYPES, by Globe Filmstrips, 1975. 1 filmstrip (59 fr.) color. (with phonorecord or cassette) Coronet Instructional Media.
Introduces the concepts of social role, sex role and stereotypes and examines their influence on attitudes and actions.

388 MALE/FEMALE: CHANGING LIFESTYLES, Educational Audio Visual, Inc., n.d. 4 filmstrips. color. (4 cassettes or phonorecords) Educational Audio Visual.
Examines the roles of men and women through history. The series is divided into four parts: Part 1, Biology and Behavior, Part 2, The Old Traditions (examines the historical roles of men and women), Part 3, Modern Trends (the impact of today's women's movement), Part 4, Young People Speak for Themselves.

389 MASCULINITY AND FEMININITY, Guidance Associates, n.d. 2 filmstrips (2 cassettes or records) color. Guidance Associates.
The concepts of masculinity and femininity are examined. An experiment in role reversal, a discussion of classic sexual stereotypes, the weighing of biological factors and cultural pressures are some of the issues covered.

390 NONTRADITIONAL CAREERS FOR WOMEN, by Pathescope Educational Media, 1974. 2 filmstrips (84-89 fr., 13 min. ea.) color. (with phonorecord or cassette) Pathescope Educational Media.
A history of women's role in the United States job market from the mid 1800's to the present, when a growing number of women hold jobs not traditionally open to them.
Review: Booklist, March 1, 1975, p683 ("Using taped comments from women holding jobs not normally thought of as 'ladies' work,' this set investigates some of the results of the current women's lib movement in terms of the ways in which women have begun to equalize the high percentage of jobs traditionally held by men").

391 PORTRAITS, by Tele KETICS, n.d. 1 filmstrip (96 fr.) color. (with phonorecord) Tele KETICS.
Presents four women from different lifestyles who are "getting it together." Interviews and visual portraits of a black social worker, a young career woman, the wife of a young politician and a divorced mother of four provide insight into the professional and personal contribution of women in society.

392 RE-EXAMINING SEX ROLES: EVOLUTION OR REVOLUTION?, by Jacoby/Storm Productions, 1975. 6 filmstrips (71-84 fr.), 15-17 min. each) color. b/w. (with cassettes) Harper & Row, Publishers.

Examines the current flux of sex roles in contemporary society. Uses graphics and interviews.

Reviews: Previews, September 1976, p30 ("In content this series is well organized and the visuals and sounds are of high quality.... Unfortunately, this series is much too broad in scope, and eclectic and nondirective in approach ... [with] no real penetration into any of the topics.... The series cannot stand alone or be used successfully by individuals not thoroughly familiar with the subject"--Elise Wendel). Media and Method, October 1975, p72; Booklist, May 1, 1976, p1280.

393 REMARKABLE AMERICAN WOMEN WHO INFLUENCED OUR LIVES, by Eye Gate Media, 1978. 6 filmstrips. color. (with cassettes)

The story of famous women including Phyllis Wheatley, a black slave who became a poet, Elizabeth Blackwell, America's first woman doctor, and Mary Katherine Goddard, the woman who printed the Declaration of Independence. The series consists of (1) Women Who Pioneered in Medicine, (2) Women Who Pioneered in Politics, (3) Women Who Pioneered in the Arts, (4) Women Who Pioneered in Business, (5) Women Who Pioneered in Journalism, (6) Women Who Pioneered in Science.

394 SEXISM IN SCHOOL: WHAT CAN WE DO?, by Activity Records, 1976. 1 filmstrip (72 fr., 15 min.) color. (with cassette) Educational Activities.

Discusses sexism in schools and examines ways in which teachers can eliminate sexist practices, materials.

395 THOSE WESTERING WOMEN, by Educational Audio Visual, n.d. 1 filmstrip (1 cassette or phonorecord) color. Educational Audio Visual.

Portrays the frontier life of the women who went West. Paintings and photographs are used to show the lives of the women--from suffragists to dance hall women.

396 TO BE A WOMAN AND A WRITER, by Guidance Associates, n.d. 2 filmstrips (2 cassettes & phonorecords) color. Guidance Associates.

Readings from literary works, literary analysis and social background provide information on the women writers of the 19th and 20th centuries. Some of the authors included are Charlotte Brontë, George Eliot, Jane Austen, Tillie Olsen, Gwendolyn Brooks, Doris Lessing, Virginia Woolf, Lorraine Hansberry and Anais Nin.

397 WHO AM I?, by Tele KETICS, n.d. 1 filmstrip (54 fr., 8 min.) (with phonorecord) Tele KETICS.

Visuals of women and feminine symbols counterpoint statements by men about women and women's role in society. The result is an insight into male and female stereotypes.

398 WILLA CATHER: REBEL FROM RED CLOUD, by Educational Audio Visual, n.d. 1 filmstrip (1 cassette or phonorecord) color. Educational Audio Visual.
Illustrations of Cather's native Nebraska show her early life and her years of struggle to gain recognition. The illustrations and narration include archival material from the Willa Cather Memorial Foundation.

399 WINGS OF CHANGE, by Media Systems Consultants, 1975. 1 filmstrip (131 fr.) color. (with phonorecord or cassette) Perfection Form Company.
Traces the development of legislation and custom concerning women in the United States from colonial times to the proposal of the 27th amendment to the Constitution. Emphasizes the early years when women campaigned for suffrage and discusses modern feminists.

400 A WOMAN'S PLACE, by Carol Tauris, n.d. 4 filmstrips (4 cassettes or phonorecords) color. Prentice-Hall Media.
An examination of the current status of women in society. Areas discussed are biological differences between men and women, myths and stereotypes related to women, the progress of the women's movement, and examples of conflict situations resulting from changes in roles, rights, and the legal status of women.

401 WOMEN!, by Prentice-Hall Media, n.d. 10 filmstrips (10 cassettes) color. Prentice-Hall Media.
A series of four units: Part 1 Struggle for Their Bodies, Part 2 In Business (job problems and discrimination), Part 3 On Their Own (why women live alone), Part 4 Women Talk About Change (the women's liberation movement).

402 WOMEN: AN AMERICAN HISTORY, by Encyclopaedia Britannica Educational Corporation, 1976. 6 filmstrips. color. (with phonorecords) Encyclopaedia Britannica.
The strips trace 350 years in the history of the American woman, from her colonial role as a valued helpmate who was legally a "non-person" to the many faceted woman of the 1970's. The set traces the evolution of women in America and explains those forces which brought change. The set includes Women of the New York, The Nice Girl and the Lady, The Fight for Equality., A Combination of Work and Hope, Beyond the Vote, and The Modern Woman's Movement.

403 WOMEN AND MEN/PEOPLE: A HISTORICAL VIEW OF CHANGING IDEAS, by Lion's Den Associates, 1976. 6 filmstrips. color. (with cassettes) Eye Gate Media.

Includes: (1) Women's Struggle for Recognition, (2) Today's Woman, (3) Woman's View of Man, (4) Man's View of Woman, (5) Different but Equal, (6) Men and Women in Groups. Examines the changing roles of men and women.

404 WOMEN AT WORK: CHOICE AND CHALLENGE, by Guidance Associates, 1975. 2 filmstrips (88 fr. and 106 fr.) color. (with phonorecords or cassettes) Guidance Associates.
Explores the changing roles of women in the work force and the challenges that these changes have generated. (Part I) Summarizes the development of women's work roles during important periods of American history. (Part 2) Offers interviews with working women and their spouses, coworkers, and children in order to provide insights into the effects of work on women.

405 WOMEN IN AMERICAN HISTORY, by Doreen Rappaport and Susan Kempler, n.d. 6 filmstrips (phonorecord or cassettes) color. Educational Activities, Inc.
Women's struggle for justice and equality and their contributions to American life are presented through vignettes from the lives of outstanding women and brief excerpts from their speeches and writings.

406 WOMEN IN LITERATURE, by Educational Audio Visual, 1976. 4 filmstrips (72-86 fr.) (with phonorecords or cassettes) Educational Audio Visual.
The filmstrips are entitled: (1) Early Literary Images, (2) The Church and the Castle, (3) The Proper Heroine, (4) Changing Images of Today. Examines the interpretation of women's roles in literature and presents the related image of women in art throughout history.
Review: Booklist, January 15, 1977, p733 ("This set sees that as women have become more influential in literature, the female image has refused to fit into any stereotyped mold and has reflected modern women's awareness of themsleves as individuals"--Beth Ann Herbert).

407 WOMEN IN THE AMERICAN REVOLUTION: LEGEND AND REALITY, by Multi Media Productions, 1975. 2 filmstrips (80 fr., 20 min. each) color. (with phonorecord or cassettes) Multi Media Productions.
The roles of colonial women, of patriots and loyalists, and Indian women in the American Revolution are presented.
Review: Previews, October 1975, p46 ("Intelligent and narratively sophisticated and informative. It indicts historians who have omitted the history of colonial woman" --Renee Feinberg).

Women's Nonprint Media 64

408 WOMEN IN THEATRE, by Olesen, n.d. 3 filmstrips (3 cassettes) color. Olesen.
Part I, The Script, surveys characteristics of women as depicted in scripts written by men and shows the way women have been viewed and portrayed through history. Part II, On the Stage, traces acting as a career with details on the lives of several famous actresses. Part III, In the Wings, surveys the contribution of women as playwrights, producers, and directors--from the 10th century to modern times.

409 WOMEN PIONEERS, by Educational Activities Records, 1976. 4 filmstrips (58-65 fr., 11-16 min. each) (with cassettes) Educational Activities Records.
The filmstrips are entitled: (1) Women in Sports, (2) Women in Medicine, (3) Women in Politics, (4) Women in Transportation. Each filmstrip is introduced by a woman pioneer in the fields of medicine, sports, politics, and transportation. Six active and successful contemporary women representing a cross-section of ages, specialties and geographical locations are featured in each filmstrip.

410 WOMEN TODAY, by Guidance Associates, n.d. 2 filmstrips (2 cassettes or phonorecords) color. Guidance Associates.
Actual interviews and dramatized sequences with leaders of the women's movement demonstrate what it is like to be a woman today. Interviews with Jane Howard, author of A Different Woman, an Acomo Indian on tribal sisterhood, and other women with a variety of life styles.

411 WOMEN WRITERS: PART 1, FANNY BURNEY TO KATE CHOPIN; PART 2, THE TWENTIETH CENTURY, n.d. 2 filmstrips (2 cassettes) color. Women's Audio Exchange.
A survey of literature from one of the first English woman novelists, Fanny Burney, through present-day writers such as Toni Morrison and Joyce Carol Oates.

412 WOMEN WRITERS: VOICES OF DISSENT, by Teaching Resources Films, 1975. 3 filmstrips (62-67 fr., 6-19 min. each) (with phonorecords or cassettes) Teaching Resources Films.
Describes the lives of Edith Wharton, Ellen Glasgow, and Willa Cather.
Review: Booklist, September 1976, p48 ("combines discerning facts about three pioneering authors with a documentary on the feminine struggle for individual freedom in the late 19th and early 20th centuries"--Beth Ames Herbert).

413 WOMEN'S WORK: AMERICA 1620-1920, by Prentice-Hall Media, n.d. 4 filmstrips (4 cassettes or phonorecords) color. Prentice-Hall Media.

Examines the history of the women's movement from colonial times through the 1920's. Outlines the influence of religion, labor, and the abolitionist movement on today's feminism.

SLIDES

414 ART OF ELIZABETH VIGEE-LEBRUN, by American Library Color Slide Company, n.d. 9 slides. color. American Library Color Slide Company.
 Works represented are: Portrait of Artist's Daughter, Portrait of Artist's Daughter as a Child, Portrait of Marquise de Jaucourt, Portrait of Lady with Wreath, Portrait of Marie Antoinette, Portait of Marie Caroline, Queen of Naples, Portrait of Princess de Talleyrand-Perigord, Self-Portrait, Self-Portrait with Daughter.

415 THE ART OF GEORGIA O'KEEFFE, by American Library Color Slide Company, n.d. 19 slides. color. American Library Color Slide Company.
 Works represented are: Black Iris, Black Spot No. 2, Blue I (watercolor), Corn Dark, Cow's Skull, Red, White and Blue, Cow's Skull with Roses, Dark Mesa, From the Lake, Green Mountains, Canada, Horse with Red Rose, Only One, Peach and Glass, Radiator Building Night, Ranchos Church, Red Hills and Bones, Seascape, Stables, Three Small Rocks Big, and White Canadian Barn.

416 THE ART OF I. RICE PEREIRA, by American Library Color Slide Company, n.d. 4 slides. color. American Library Color Slide Company.
 Paintings represented are: Blue Wind, Celestial Gate Sways on Ringing Swells, Green Depth, and Rose Flux.

417 THE ART OF IRENE ZEVON, by American Library Color Slide Company, n.d. 30 sides. color. American Library Color Slide Company.
 Thirty paintings of the artist are represented.

418 ART OF MARION GREENWOOD, by American Library Color Slide Company, n.d. 3 slides. color. American Library Color Slide Company.
 Works represented are: Ceremonial Dance, New Year's Eve, and Rehearsal, African Ballet.

419 ART OF MARY BAUERMEISTER, by American Library Color Slide Company, n.d. 2 slides. color. American Library Color Slide Company.

The two paintings represented are Homage to Marbert Du Breer (1964), New York, the Whitney Museum, and Integration (1964) in a private collection in New York.

420 THE ART OF MARY CASSATT, by American Library Color Slide Company, n.d. 23 slides. color. American Library Color Slide Company.
Works represented are: The Bath, Boating Party, Cup of Tea, In Country, Lady at Tea Table, Loge, Lydia Cassatt Reading in a Garden, Maternity, Morning Toilet, Mother and Child (there are 3: in the Chicago Art Institute, Washington National Gallery, and New York Brooklyn Museum), Mother and Child in Bed, On the Water, Portrait of Elderly Lady, Portrait of Mary Ellison, Study for Banjo Lesson, Woman with Dog, Woman with Red Carnation, Women and Child, Young Girl, Young Mother Sewing, Young Wife.

421 ART OF PEGGY BACON, by American Library Color Slide Company, n.d. 1 slide, color. American Library Color Slide Company.
The painting Nobody's Pet by Peggy Bacon (b. 1905), which is dated 1938 and is in the artist's personal collection, is represented.

422 THE ART OF PEARL GUENTHER, by American Color Slide Company, n.d. 6 slides. color. American Library Color Slide Company.
The works represented are: Blue Umbrella, Good Book, The Jungfrau, Switzerland, Our Porch at Oceanside, Our Porch and St. Malo Roofs, and White Water Canyon.

423 THE ART OF PERLE FINE, by American Library Color Slide Company, n.d. 7 slides. color. American Library Color Slide Company.
The paintings represented are: Cool Blue, Cold Green: No. 29 (1961), private collection; Key (collage), 1961, collection of artist; Mute and Aloof: No. 11 (1961), collection of the artist; Noon in July (1960), collection of the artist; Radiance at Noon (collage), 1959, collection of the artist; Rough Hewn, No. 36 (1962), collection of the artist; Study for Ritual (1961), collection of the artist.

424 ART OF SUE FULLER, by American Library Color Slide Company, n.d. 1 slide. color. American Library Color Slide Company.
Work represented is String Composition No. 119 (1964), New York, private collection.

425 [ART WORKS OF WOMEN ARTISTS], by Dr. Alan Garfield, n.d. 2478 slides. Dr. Alan Garfield.

The collection is mainly historical, with special emphasis given to Baroque women painters, printmakers and sculptors and Surrealist women painters.

426 BERTHE MORISOT--DRAWINGS, by American Library Color Slide Company, n.d. 10 slides. American Library Color Slide Company.

427 BERTHE MORISOT--PAINTINGS, by American Library Color Slide Company, n.d. 10 slides. American Library Color Slide Company.

428 BERTHE MORISOT--PASTELS, by American Library Color Slide Company, n.d. 10 slides. American Library Color Slide Company.

429 THE BIRTH CONTROL THING, by Elizabeth Walker, 1976. Slides (15 min.) color. (with cassette) Douglas College.
Begins with a survey of the methods of birth control used throughout history. Men and women of all ages talk about the many different ways and means of birth control they have used and the effects they have encountered, both physically and psychologically.

430 THE COOPTATION OF THE WOMEN'S MOVEMENT IN ADVERTISING, by Women's Research Project, n.d. 20 slides. color, b/w (script). Women's Film Coop.
Shows how advertising uses the women's movement to sell their products. The Virginia Slims commercial is just one example.

431 DICK AND JANE AS VICTIMS, by Women on Words and Images, n.d. 140 slides (cassette) Women on Words and Images.
The slides document the extensive sex-role stereotyping in children's readers. Activeness and bravery in boys is contrasted with passivity and frailty in girls. The stereotypical treatment of adults also is presented.

432 EDITH BRY--PAINTING, by American Library Color Slide Company, n.d. 10 slides. American Library Color Slide Company.

433 FAMOUS PAINTINGS BY WOMEN ARTISTS, by American Library Color Slide Company, n.d. 55 slides. American Library Color Slide Company.
European and American women artists.

434 GE SLIDE SHOW, by Women's Research Project, n.d. 56 slides. color, b/w (script). Women's Film Coop.

Slides combine General Electric promotional material with visual and narrative investigations of General Electric's global manipulations of women and poor people through both consumer indoctrination and economic imperialism.

435 GEORGIA O'KEEFFE--PAINTING, by American Library Color Slide Company, n.d. 10 slides. American Library Color Slide Company.

436 HELEN GERARDIA--PAINTING, by American Library Color Slide Company, n.d. 10 slides. American Library Color Slide Company.

437 HELP WANTED: SEXISM IN CAREER EDUCATION MATERIALS, by Women on Words and Images, 1975. 140 slides. color. (with cassette) Women on Words and Images.
Examination of sexism in career related materials. Includes suggestions for creative neutralizing of sexism in the classroom.

438 HOW FAR DO YOU HAVE TO GO?, by Ann Bishop and Isabel Gordon, 1974. Slides (11 min.) color. (with cassette)
Asks the question, "How much must a female worker compromise herself to get or keep a job?" What kind of reasons for not being hired or for being fired constitute discrimination under the human rights code?

439 INTERNATIONAL WOMEN'S YEAR TRIBUNE--MEXICO 1975, by Vicke Semler and Ann Walker, 1976. 80 slides. color. (with cassette) Douglas College.
Report of IWY Tribune, held in June 1975 in Mexico City. The major themes and issues of the Tribune are presented.

440 IS ANATOMY DESTINY?: WOMEN IN AMERICA, by Multi Media Productions, 1974. 53 slides. color. Multi Media Productions.
Explores the roles of women in American society as housewives and as members of the American work force.
Review: Booklist, November 1, 1975, p399 ("A most objective presentation of women and their roles in society as housewives and economic competitors in the job market").

441 MAN AND WOMAN: MYTHS AND STEREOTYPES, by Center for Humanities, 1974. 160 slides. color. b/w. (with cassette) Center for Humanities.
Examines the myths and stereotypes about men and women that underlie our culture.

Women's Nonprint Media   70

Review: Previews, April 1976, p38 ("This striking, entertaining, and thought-provoking selection of visual and sound images has tremendous potential"--Judith Schmidt).

442 MARY CASSATT--PAINTING, by American Library Color Slide Company, n.d. 10 slides. American Library Color Slide Company.

443 MAYBE NEXT TIME, by Nomi Promislow and Merrill Fearon, 1974. Slides (10 min.) color. (with cassette) Douglas College.

About a female tree planter who doesn't get a contract because there are no toilet facilities for women on the site.

444 AN OLD STORY, by Martha Miller, 1975. Slides. (15 min.) color. (with cassette) Douglas College.

Three women candidly discuss their menopause. The three women, all of different sensibilities, express remarkably similar feelings.

445 PAINTINGS BY 19th AND 20TH CENTURY WOMEN ARTISTS, by The American Library Color Slide Company, 1976. 35 slides. color. The American Library Color Slide Company.

Works by O'Keeffe, Valaden, Pereira, Leyster, et al.

446 PIONEER WOMEN, by Susan Sutherland, 1974. Slides. (16 min.) b/w. (with cassette) Douglas College.

A visual montage of original photographs of British Columbia women around the turn of the century.

447 RECOVERING OUR PAST: THE STRUGGLE FOR WOMEN'S SUFFRAGE, by the Feminist History Research Project, 1975. 80 slides. (with cassette) Feminist History Research Project.

Combines the recorded voices of women who participated in the struggle for suffrage with photographs and engravings of the period.

Reviews: Previews, September 1976, p32 ("splendidly organized and most valuable bit of oral history"; "good for the scholar and ... for young people to see the foundations of suffering and struggle on which present efforts must build"--Janet Polacheck). Media and Methods, February 1975, p43. Media Mix, February 1975, p6.

448 THE RE-EDUCATION OF WOMEN AND MEN: CREATING NEW RELATIONSHIPS, by The Center for Humanities, 1976. 160 slides, color. (with phonorecords or cassette) Center for Humanities.

Considers the physical, emotional, and intellectual abilities of women and examines specific relationship situations which raise questions about conventional sex roles.

Slides

449 THE ROLE OF WOMEN IN B.C.'S HISTORY, by Ann Hogan, 1973. 2 slide sets. (set 1, 67 slides, set 2, 217 slides) b/w. Douglas College.
Set 1 is entitled The Role of Women in B.C. to 1914. The slides provide information on every facet of women's lives in pioneer British Columbia. Set 2 is entitled History of Women's Work in B.C. 1914-1950. The set is divided into several sections. Each section covers a specific subject such as the Vancouver Woman's Building, the suffragette movement, the first woman taxi driver, etc.

450 SALUTE TO ALICE PAUL, by Feminist Productions, 1977. Slides. (15 min.) color. (with cassette) Feminist Productions.
A documentary about Alice Paul, the author of the Equal Rights Amendment.

451 SEXISM IN FOREIGN LANGUAGE TEXTBOOKS, by Women on Words and Images, n.d. 140 slides (cassette) Women on Words and Images.
Explores the sexist content of 25 foreign textbooks by 16 publishers.

452 SEXIST LANGUAGE, by Feminist Productions, 1977. Slides. (30 min.) color. (with cassette) Feminist Productions.
Presentation demonstrating that sexist language leads to and perpetuates the devaluation and oppression of women.

453 SISTER, by Mo Simpson, 1975. Slides (10 min.) color. (with cassette) Douglas College.
A celebration of sisterhood. Most of the photographs were taken and the music recorded at the Western Canadian Women's Festival, Spring, 1975.

454 VIOLENCE IN THE FAMILY: THE SECRET TRAGEDY, by Human Relations Media Center, 1979. 240 slides. color. (with cassette or phonorecord) Center for the Humanities, Inc.
A three-part program exploring the underlying causes of violence in the family. Part 1 deals with the nature of violence. The effects of the changing role of women on family violence is examined. Part 2 concentrates on child abuse and neglect. Part 3 investigates marital violence; when, where, and why wife beating occurs and the complex reasons why women stay in such relationships are examined.

455 WHAT CAN MOTHER DO FOR MOTHER?, by Roberta Kalazirou, 1976. Slides. (14 min.) color. (with cassette) Douglas College.

A personal account of a mother with a small child. Examines what changes that becoming a mother has made on her marriage and her need to be a more fulfilled woman. Looks at mother-child programs such as Family Place, an innovative family resource center in British Columbia.

456 A WOMAN'S PLACE, by Nomi Promislow and Merrill Fearon, 1974. Slides. (8 min.) color. (with cassette) Douglas College.
When a married woman decides to apply for a loan to purchase a car, she is unaware of the problems she will have to contend with because she is a woman.

457 WOMEN AND ALCOHOLISM, by Feminist Productions, 1977. Slides. (30 min.) color. (with cassette) Feminist Productions.
Presentation concerning the causes, problems and treatment of women alcoholics.

458 [WOMEN ARTISTS], by Rosenthal Art Slides, n.d. app. 260 slides. Rosenthal Art Slides.
The company publishes a two-volume catalog of their collection of about 22,000 slides. Indexes are available also. Index XIV, Women Artists, provides an alphabetical listing of women artists included in the catalog and the slide collection. The index is divided into two categories, Pre-20th Century and 20th Century. Approximately 260 artists (with media indicated) are represented in the index and the slide collection.

459 WOMEN ARTISTS: A HISTORICAL SURVEY (EARLY MIDDLE AGES TO 1900), by Harper & Row, 1975. 120 slides. color. (with notes and index) Harper & Row.
Review: Booklist, November 1, 1976, p365-366 ("Surveys the accomplishments of women artists whose works and styles may be unfamiliar due to the sexual prejudice that appears to be common to the arts as well as to the more traditional professions"--Janice Bolt).

460 WOMEN ARTISTS: 1550-1950, by the Los Angeles County Museum of Art, 1977. 61 slides. color. Rosenthal Art Slides.
A series of slides of the 1977 exhibit Women Artists: 1550-1950, at the Los Angeles County Museum of Art. A catalog is available which corresponds to the slides. Forty-five artists are represented.

461 WOMEN ARTISTS: IMAGES--THEMES AND DREAMS, by Harper & Row, 1975. 80 slides. color. (with notes and index) Harper & Row.
Presents views of sculpture and paintings by women artists, illustrating common themes in women's art. Artists

included are Mary Cassatt, Audrey Flack, Leonor Fini, Barbara Hepworth, Marisol, Charley Toorap, Remedios Varo and Suzanne Valadon.

462 WOMEN ARTISTS: THE TWENTIETH CENTURY, by Harper & Row, 1975. 80 slides. color. (with notes and index) Harper & Row.
Presents views of paintings and sculpture by European and American women of the 20th century.

463 WOMEN ARTISTS: THIRD WORLD, by Harper & Row, 1975. 80 slides, color, (with notes and index) Harper & Row.
Presents views of paintings and sculpture by American women of African, Japanese, Chinese and Mexican descent.

464 WOMEN IN CHINA, by Mo Simpson and Mary Jane Cowan, 1975. Slides. (15 min.) color. b/w. (with cassette) Douglas College.
This slide/sound presentation, through music, interviews, and narration, traces women's advancement in the context of China's political and social revolution. Women discuss their equality in terms of marriage, employment, and education.

465 WOMEN NOW, by Feminist Productions, 1975. Slides (40 min.) color. (with cassette) Feminist Productions.
Deals with questions about NOW, feminism, rape, sexuality, sisterhood, consciousness raising, ERA, marriage, and other issues of concern to women.

466 A WOMEN'S HISTORY SLIDE SHOW, by the Cambridge-Goddard Feminist History Project, n.d. 450 slides. color. b/w. (with script) Women's Film Coop.
The slides portray average white, western, working class women throughout history. They are divided into four sections: Medieval England, 17th Century in England, 19th Century and Women in Revolt.

RECORDINGS/SPOKEN WORD

467 ABORTION REPORT, by Feminist Radio Network, n.d. cassette or reel-to-reel. (59 min.) Feminist Radio Network.
A speaker from the American Civil Liberties Union, Nellie Gray of the March for Life, a clinic nurse, and activists including Gloria Steinem present a full discussion of the issues.

468 ADOLESCENT PUBERTY RITUALS, by Pacifica Tape Library, 1972. cassette or reel-to-reel. (39 min.) Pacifica Tape Library.
Women discuss the problems and frustrations of growing up; including the conditioning and rituals disguised as "preparation for womanhood."

469 AIN'T IT A SHAME: BATTERED WOMEN, by Feminist Radio Network, n.d. cassette or reel-to-reel (29 min.) Feminist Radio Network.
Victims of woman-abuse, with feminist activists and attorneys, discuss how woman-abuse is rooted in the sexism and violence of our culture. New alternatives like shelter houses and support groups are also discussed.

470 ALICE WALKER, by Arlene Acker, n.d. cassette or reel-to-reel (28 min.) Feminist Radio Network.
Alice Walker, author of "Evolutionary Petunia and Other Poems," talks about being a black woman and writer.

471 AMAZON WOMEN, by Pacifica Tape Library, 1976. cassette or reel-to-reel. (54 min.) Pacifica Tape Library.
Janet Siskind, Rutgers University professor of anthropology, shares insights from her book, To Hunt in the Morning, based on her experiences with the men and women of the Sheninoa, a primitive tribe of tropical forest Indians in Peru.

472 ANAIS NIN, by Everett/Edwards, Inc., n.d. cassette Everett/Edwards, Inc.
Narration by Philip Jason.

Recordings/Spoken Word

473 ANGELINE AND SARAH GIMKE, by Pacifica Tape Library, 1962. Cassette or reel-to-reel (30 min.) Pacifica Tape Library.
These two sisters were the only Southern white women in the abolitionist movement.

474 AMELIA EARHART/THE FIRST WOMAN TO FLY THE ATLANTIC SOLO, by Mark 56. phonorecord. Ladyslipper Music.
Amelia Earhart, her sister, and others talk about aviation and Miss Earhart's ambitions and interests.

475 AMERICAN WOMEN IN HISTORY, by Pacifica Tape Library, n.d. Cassette or reel-to-reel (65 min.) Pacifica Tape Library.
Isabel Welsh of the University of California at Berkeley talks about the political thought of Ann Hutchinson, Abigail Adams, Jane Addams, Emma Goldman, and others.

476 ANNE SEXTON, by Everett/Edwards, Inc., n.d. cassette. Everett/Edwards, Inc.
Narration by Rivkah Feldman.

477 AN ANTHROPOLOGICAL PERSPECTIVE, by Everett/Edwards, Inc., n.d. cassette. Everett/Edwards, Inc.
Narration by Ruby R. Leavitt.

478 Austen, Jane. EMMA, n.d. cassette. Everett/Edwards Inc.
Discussion of the story "Emma" by George H. Ford.

479 Austen, Jane. MANSFIELD PARK, n.d. cassette. Everett/Edwards, Inc.
Discussion of "Mansfield Park" by A.M. Duckworth.

480 Austen, Jane. NORTHANGER ABBEY, n.d. cassette. Everett/Edwards, Inc.

481 Austen, Jane. PERSUASION, n.d. cassette. Everett/Edwards, Inc.
Discussion of this work by Stuart M. Tave.

482 Austen, Jane. PRIDE AND PREJUDICE, n.d. cassette. Everett/Edwards, Inc.
Discussion by A. Walton Litz.

483 Austen, Jane. SENSE AND SENSIBILITY, n.d. cassette. Everett/Edwards, Inc.
Discussion by Stephen Parrish.

484 THE AWAKENING OF KATE CHOPIN, n.d. cassette. Everett/Edwards, Inc.
A study of the work of Kate Chopin by Linda K. Kuehl.

485 THE BLACK WOMAN IN AMERICA, by Pacifica Tape Library, 1968. Cassette or reel-to-reel (51 min.) Pacifica Tape Library.
A discussion about the problems facing the black woman. It features such women as Peachie Brooks, Verta Smart Grosvenor, Flo Kennedy, and Elinor Norton.

486 BLACK WOMEN IN AMERICA, n.d. cassette. Women's Audio Exchange.
Two cassettes. Part 1 is "The History of Oppression from the Distaff Side." Part 2 is "The Civil War Ends and Another War Begins."

487 BLACK WOMEN IN AMERICA, by Pacifica Tape Library, 1974. Cassette or reel-to-reel (46 min.) Pacifica Tape Library.
A speech by Angela Davis on the struggles and accomplishments of black and other minority women.

488 BLACK WOMEN WRITERS, by Everett/Edwards, Inc. n.d. cassette. Everett/Edwards.
Narration by Pat Exum.

489 BLACK WOMEN'S SPEECHES, by Folkways, n.d. phonorecord. Ladyslipper Music.
Ruby Dee reads famous speeches by black women. In two volumes.

490 BONNY RAITT, by Red Tape, n.d. cassette or reel-to-reel (29 min.) Feminist Radio Network.
Bonnie talks about blues, the music which has influenced her work, and explains what it's like as a woman with some political consciousness in the music industry.

491 Brontë, Charlotte. JANE EYRE. n.d. cassette. Everett/Edwards, Inc.
Comments by Vineta Colby.

492 BUT THE WOMEN ROSE, VOL. 1 and 2, by Folkways, n.d. phonorecord. Rounder Records.

493 CENTURY OF STRUGGLE AND ENTERPRISING WOMEN, n.d. cassette. Woman's Audio Exchange.
Caroline Bird and Eleanor Flexner discuss the feminist movement and issues concerning women of this century.

Recordings/Spoken Word

494 THE CHANGING LIVES OF WOMEN AROUND THE GLOBE, by Pacifica Tape Library, 1971. cassette or reel-to-reel (70 min.) Pacifica Tape Library.
An examination of the changes in women's lives in India, Japan, Mexico and Sweden. Also included are some Eastern European countries.

495 CHANGING ROLES OF MALES AND FEMALES, by Everett/Edwards, Inc. n.d. cassette. Everett/Edwards, Inc.
Narration by Margaret Mead.

496 CHILDHOOD OF FAMOUS WOMEN, by H.W. Wilson Corporation, n.d. cassette. H.W. Wilson Corporation.
Biographies of Edna St. Vincent Millay, Marie Curie, Louisa May Alcott, and Annie Sullivan.
Review: Previews, November 1976, p35 ("describes the motivation behind the later successes of these women"-- Darlene Weston).

497 CHRISTINE DE PISAN, by Everett/Edwards, Inc., n.d. cassette. Everett/Edwards, Inc.
Narration by Diane Bornstein.

498 COLETTE, by Everett/Edwards, Inc., n.d. cassette. Everett/Edwards, Inc.
Narration by Elaine Marks.

499 CONTEMPORARY WOMEN'S MOVEMENT, by Everett/Edwards, n.d. cassette. Everett/Edwards, Inc.
Narration by Judith Papachristou.

500 A CONVERSATION WITH CINDY NEMSER, by Pacifica Tape Library, 1975. Cassette or reel-to-reel (49 min.) Pacifica Tape Library.
Editor of the Feminist Art Journal traces the difficulties that led to her publishing the journal. Discusses the importance of the feminist movement for establishing the climate so women artists are able to be independent. Uses Louise Nevelson, Ava Hesse, and Audrey Flack as examples.

501 CONVERSATION WITH MARJORIE ROSEN, by Pacifica Tape Library, n.d. cassette or reel-to-reel. (58 min.) Pacifica Tape Library.
Film critic Marjorie Rosen discusses her views of current films. She would like to see a more adequate representation of women in film, and feels women have been stereotyped in film as well as in everyday life.

502 COURAGEOUS SISTERS, by Pacifica Tape Library, n.d. Cassette or reel-to-reel. (60 min.) Pacifica Tape Library.

Dramatized speeches, music, and diaries of the important women of the 19th century. Also a discussion with Isabel Welsh, historian.

503 DEAR DOCTOR AIN'T SO DEAR, by Pacifica Tape Library, n.d. Cassette or reel-to-reel. (62 min.) Pacifica Tape Library.
A criticism of the United States medical profession from the feminist viewpoint.

504 DEPRESSION IN MIDDLE AGE, by Everett/Edwards, Inc., n.d. cassette. Everett/Edwards, Inc.
Narration by Pauline Bart.

505 DIANE WAKOSKI: AN INTERVIEW, by Everett/Edwards, Inc., n.d. cassette. Everett/Edwards, Inc.
Interview by Elaine H. Baruch.

506 DIANE WAKOSKI READS HER WORK, by Everett/Edwards, Inc., n.d. cassette. Everett/Edwards.
Selections read by the author.

507 DISCUSSION WITH WOMEN, n.d. cassette. Women's Audio Exchange.
Among the issues discussed with Dr. Nathaniel Branden are marital fidelity, bi-sexuality, masculine-feminine role playing, ideal marriage age, male impotence, female orgasm, infatuation, the significance of sexual fantasy, emotional repression in marriage, and many other topics.

508 DO WORKING GIRLS LEAD A GLAMOROUS LIFE?, by Pacifica Tape Library, 1976. Cassette or reel-to-reel. (55 min.) Pacifica Tape Library.
Interviews with prostitutes, Margot St. James (an organizer of prostitutes) and Dr. Harold Greenwald, author of The Call Girl.

509 DORIS LESSING READS HER SHORT STORIES, n.d. cassette. Women's Audio Exchange.
[No description available.]

510 DOROTHEA DICKS, by Pacifica Tape Library, 1962. Cassette or reel-to-reel. (32 min.) Pacifica Tape Library.
One of the first people to work for reforming the way the insane were treated in prison. She also organized nurses for the Civil War.

511 THE DRIVE FOR SUFFRAGE, by Everett/Edwards, Inc., n.d. cassette. Everett/Edwards, Inc.
Narration by Judith Papachristou.

512 EARLY EUROPEAN FEMINISTS, by Everett/Edwards, Inc., n.d. cassette. Everett/Edwards, Inc.
Narration by Susan G. Bell.

513 EILEEN GREY: ARCHITECT, by Pacifica Tape Library, 1975. Cassette or reel-to-reel (55 min.) Pacifica Tape Library.
Susanna Torres and Debby Nevins recall the history of Eileen Grey's work with Le Corbusier and her subsequent problems with discrimination.

514 Eliot, George. ADAM BEDE, n.d. cassette. Everett/Edwards, Inc.
Comments by V.C. Knoepflmacher.

515 Eliot, George. MIDDLEMARCH, n.d. cassette. Everett/Edwards, Inc.
Discussion by George H. Ford.

516 Eliot, George. THE MILL ON THE FLOSS, n.d. cassette. Everett/Edwards, Inc.
Commentary by V.C. Knoepflmacher.

517 ELIZABETH BARRETT BROWNING, n.d. cassette. Everett/Edwards, Inc.
Discussion by Ellen Moers.

518 ELIZABETH CADY STANTON AND SUSAN B. ANTHONY, by Pacifica Tape Library, 1962. cassette or reel-to-reel (28 min.) Pacifica Tape Library.
A complete portrait of these two women--not just their political activity.

519 EMILY DICKINSON, by Everett/Edwards, Inc., n.d. cassette. Everett/Edwards, Inc.
Narration by Virginia Terris.

520 EMILY DICKINSON AS A WOMAN POET, by Everett/Edwards, Inc., n.d. cassette. Everett/Edwards, Inc.
A lecture by Virginia Terris on the poetry of Emily Dickenson.

521 EMMA GOLDMAN, by Everett/Edwards, Inc., 1976. cassette. (30 min.) Everett/Edwards, Inc.
Excerpts from Emma Goldman's speeches and writings. Provides a portrait of the woman and her work.

522 EQUAL RIGHTS AMENDMENT, by Feminist Radio Network, n.d. cassette or reel-to-reel. (29 min.) Feminist Radio Network.
Traces the ERA from its beginnings to the recently granted extension of time for ratification. Ellie Smeal of

NOW discusses the impact of the ERA and both the pro and con activists explain their positions.

523 EROTIC ART BY WOMEN, by Pacifica Tape Library, 1975. Cassette or reel-to-reel. (42 min.) Pacifica Tape Library.
Five women erotic artists discuss their work, its purpose, its contrast with pornography, and its social and psychological basis.

524 Fabio, Sarah Webster. BOSS SOUL, n.d. phonorecord. Folkways Records.
Twelve poems read by Sarah Webster Fabio. Includes "Drum Talk" and "Rhythms and Images."
Review: Listening Post, January 1974.

525 Fabio, Sarah Webster. SOUL AIN'T, SOUL IS, n.d. phonorecord. Folkways Records.
Selections from the poetry of Sarah Webster Fabio read by the author.

526 FEELINGS OF LOVE NOT YET EXPRESSED, n.d. phonorecord. Women's Audio Exchange.
A collection of the "Neo-Black" women in poetry reading their own works. Read by Amirh Bahat, China Clark, and Jo Ann McKnight.

527 THE FEMALE PRISONER, by Pacifica Tape Library, 1973. cassette or reel-to-reel. (75 min.) Pacifica Tape Library.
Two women, both ex-prisoners, have a lot to say about the horror story which is the life of today's women in prison.

528 FEMALE SEXUALITY, by Vera Rosenbluth, n.d. reel-to-reel. (45 min.) Douglas College.
A discussion by three women (aged 31, 36, and 41) who talk about some of their experiences and attitudes toward their sexuality.

529 FEMINISTS' CONVERSATIONS, by Pacifica Tape Library, 1976. cassette or reel-to-reel. (60 min.) Pacifica Tape Library.
A discussion between Reyna Reiter and Jane Lazarre which explores society's "put-down" of the role of motherhood and the present ambivalence of women about becoming mothers.

530 FEMINISTS FIGHT THE PORNBROKERS, by Lani Silver, n.d. cassette or reel-to-reel. (59 min.) Feminist Radio Network.
A documentary investigating the pornography industry and examining issues such as censorship, why women

are portrayed as victims, and whether pornography leads to rape. Several interviews explore the industry from a range of perspectives.

531 FICTIONS AND TRUE STORIES: WRITING ABOUT WOMEN'S LIVES, by Chris Carroll, n.d. cassette and reel-to-reel (30 min.) Feminist Radio Network.
Maxine Kumin, Pulitzer-Prize winning poet, Grace Paley, author, and Alice Walker, short-story writer, recall some milestones from their lives and share their views about the future of women's writing.

532 THE FLIGHT FROM WOMEN, by Everett/Edwards, Inc., n.d. cassette. Everett/Edwards, Inc.
Narration by Paul Zweig.

533 FRANCES WILLARD, by Pacifica Tape Library, 1962. cassette or reel-to-reel. (24 min.) Pacifica Tape Library.
An investigation of Ms. Willard's Political School for Women and the first mass political movement for women in the United States--the temperance crusade.

534 FRANCES WRIGHT, by Pacifica Tape Library, 1962. cassette or reel-to-reel. (28 min.) Pacifica Tape Library.
A portrait of the first woman traveler in the United States to write an account; the first woman playwright to have a play produced in New York; and a pioneer in the fight for free public schools, divorce law reform, and birth control.

535 FRIENDSHIP AND LONELINESS, by Pacifica Tape Library, 1972. cassette or reel-to-reel. (42 min.) Pacifica Tape Library.
The personal testimony of the loneliness experienced by women, stemming from marriage, divorce, and a general inability to relate to the world. Women discuss various means for obtaining fulfillment and friendship.

536 FROM ONE STRUGGLE TO ANOTHER, by Pacifica Tape Library, n.d. cassette or reel-to-reel. (71 min.) Pacifica Tape Library.
Judy Chicago and Miriam Shapiro talk about the male-dominated art world of New York.

537 Gaskell, Elizabeth. MARY BARTON, n.d. cassette. Everett/Edwards, Inc.
Discussion by Coral Lansbury.

538 Gaskell, Elizabeth. NORTH AND SOUTH, n.d. cassette. Everett/Edwards, Inc.
Comments by Coral Lansbury.

Women's Nonprint Media   82

539 GEORGE SAND, by Everett/Edwards, Inc. n.d. cassette. Everett/Edwards, Inc.
Narration by Katherine Carson.

540 GERTRUDE STEIN READS FROM HER WORKS, n.d. phonorecord/cassette. Women's Audio Exchange.
Gertrude Stein reads from "The Making of Americans" (Part 1 and 2), "A Valentine for Sherwood Anderson," "If I Told Him: A Completed Portrait of Picasso," "Matisse," and "Madame Recamier: An Opera."

541 Giovanni, Nikki. LEGACIES/THE POETRY OF NIKKI GIOVANNI, by Folkways Records, 1976. phonorecord. Folkways Records.
Selections read by Nikki Giovanni are "Once a Lady Told Me," "Conversation," "The Genie in the Jar," "Mothers," "The December of My Springs," "The Life I Led," "Everytime It Rains," and "Mother's Habits."

542 Hacker, Marilyn. THE POETRY AND VOICE OF..., by Caedmon Records, n.d. phonorecord. Caedmon Records.
Hacker reads her work at New York's Poetry Center.
Reviews: Previews, December 1976, p22 ("evocative and of an intellectual depth that invites repeated listening" --Margaret Bush). Booklist, February 15, 1977, p916.

543 Hansberry, Lorraine. A RAISIN IN THE SUN, by Everett/Edwards, Inc., n.d. cassette. Everett/Edwards, Inc.
Hansberry's work is discussed by C.W.E. Bigsby.

544 Hansberry, Lorraine. TO BE YOUNG, GIFTED AND BLACK, by Caedmon Records, n.d. phonorecord. Caedmon Records.
The play is the story of Lorraine Hansberry's life from her earliest childhood memories of the Chicago ghetto to the years of creative struggle and triumph.

545 HISTORIANS' NEGLECT OF WOMEN, by Everett/Edwards, n.d. cassette. Everett/Edwards, Inc.
Narration by Judith Papachristou.

546 HOLLY NEAR TODAY, by Feminist Radio Network, n.d. cassette or reel-to-reel. (29 min.) Feminist Radio Network.
An interview in which Holly talks about the power of music and musicians, the abuses of that power in the male-dominated music industry, and the growth of feminist record companies such as her label, Redwood Records.

547 HOUSEWORK, by Pacifica Tape Library, 1972. cassette or reel-to-reel. (45 min.) Pacifica Tape Library.
Different perspectives on housework are presented

as women share their views with each other. Some of the women view housework as unpaid, unappreciated labor, contributing to a loss of identity and creativity. Others see it as a vehicle to demonstrate concern for one's family and for providing self-fulfillment.

548 HOUSTON, by Lani Silver, 1977. cassette or reel-to-reel. (25 min.) Feminist Radio Network.

The tape was made at the 1977 women's conference in Houston. Some of the delegates interviewed are Bella Abzug, Betty Friedan, Gloria Steinem, Billie Jean King, Jean Stapleton, and Kate Millett. The impact of the conference as well as the conflict between conservatives and feminists as to what will be the future role of women in America are explored.

549 HOW WE FEEL ABOUT OUR BODIES I, by Pacifica Tape Library, 1972. Cassette or reel-to-reel. (52 min.) Pacifica Tape Library.

Six women relate their background and discuss such topics as attitudes toward women's bodies, adolescence, pregnancy, childbirth and menstruation.

550 HOW WE FEEL ABOUT OUR BODIES II, by Pacifica Tape Library, 1972. Cassette or reel-to-reel. (34 min.) Pacifica Tape Library.

This discusssion among six women centers on societal pressures to conform to "ideals" of feminine beauty and the concept of women as men's property.

551 I AM A WOMAN, n.d. phonorecords. Women's Audio Exchange.

Performance by Viveca Lindfors--a journey of one woman and many women. Two phonorecords.

552 THE IMAGE OF WOMEN IN ART, by Pacifica Tape Library, 1972. cassette or reel-to-reel. (78 min.) Pacifica Tape Library.

Lecture by Dr. Linda Nochlin of Vassar on the image of women.

553 IN HONOR OF MARGARET MEAD, by Pacifica Tape Library, 1978. 10 cassettes (from 23 to 102 minutes.) Pacifica Tape Library.

Ten programs from the Pacifica Archives covering a decade (1968-1978) of Dr. Mead's commentary on Culture and Human Interdependence, Changing Lifestyles, the Generation Gap, Children and Creativity, Drugs and Society, Sexual Freedom, War and Death.

554 THE ISRAELI WOMEN'S MOVEMENT, by Pacifica Tape Library, 1973. cassette or reel-to-reel. (35 min.) Pacifica Tape Library.

Describes the current consciousness-raising in Israel and traces activities of its newly developing women's movement. Presents the oppression of Israeli women and the opposition to the progressive changes for which many Israeli women are now working.

555 IT CHANGED MY LIFE, by Pacifica Tape Library, 1976. Cassette or reel-to-reel. (28 min.) Pacifica Tape Library.
Betty Friedan communicates her enthusiasm, her hopes and her fears for the women's movement in this interview based on her new book, It Changed my Life.

556 Jackson, Shirley. THE DAEMON LOVER AND THE LOTTERY, n.d. phonorecord or cassette. Folkways Records.
Two short stories read by the author, Shirley Jackson.
Review: Listening Post, April 1975, p6 ("The stories, themselves brilliant literary examples, are not done justice in this interpretation"--Dennis Petticoffer).

557 Jackson, Shirley. THE LOTTERY AND OTHER STORIES, 1976. phonorecord or cassette. (60 min.) Caedmon Records.
Shirley Jackson's short stories are read by actress Maureen Stapleton.
Review: Previews, November 1976, p36 ("Stapleton gives quietly understated readings"--James Limbacher).

558 JAZZ WOMEN: A SERIES, by Jill Schapiro, n.d. 10 cassettes or reel-to-reel. (45 & 60 min.) Feminist Radio Network.
The series includes the following: (1) A First in Jazz History--Composer/Band-Leader Toshiko Akiyoshi, (2) Pioneer of New Directions--Composer Carla Bley, (3) The Changing Eras of Jazz Survive in Mary Lou Williams, (4) Twenty Fingers--Two Modern Pianists (Marian McPartland and Patti Brown), (5) Shoo-Be-Do-Wop, etc.--Traditional Scat and Vocalise (Ella Fitzgerald, Annie Ross, Betty Carter), (6) From a Whisper to a Scream--Contemporary Scat (Flora Purim and Urszula Dudziak), (7) Grooving in the Ether--Harps (Dorothy Ashby and Alice Coltrane), (8) An Ax to Grind--Guitars (Mary Osborne and Monnette Sudler), (9) Ivory Excursions--Four Contemporary Pianists (Patrice Rushen, Jill McManus, Joanne Bracken, Jessica Williams), (10) Move Over, Gabriel--Horns (Vi Redd, Melba Liston, Barbara Donald).

559 JOAN GOULIANO'S BY A WOMAN WRIT. Pacifica Tape Library, 1974. Cassette or reel-to-reel. (61 min.) Pacifica Tape Library.

Joan Goulianos is the editor of an anthology of outstanding but largely neglected women writers of the last 600 years. The writings, personalized nonfiction, are discussed as rebellion against sexism, academic tyranny.

560 Jong, Erica. FRUITS AND VEGETABLES, HALFLIVES, LOVEROOT, AND OTHERS, n.d. phonorecord or cassette. Women's Audio Exchange.
Also includes excerpts from Fear of Flying read by Erica Jong.

561 THE KITCHEN SINK PAPERS, by Pacifica Tape Library, 1975. Cassette or reel-to-reel. (57 min.) Pacifica Tape Library.
Mike McGrady is the author of The Kitchen Sink Papers. This interview with McGrady and his wife reveals the changes in their lives brought about when he and his wife exchanged places for one year.

562 LEADERSHIP AND POWER, by Everett/Edwards, Inc. n.d. cassette. Everett/Edwards.
Narration by Eleanor Zuckerman.

563 LEE BROWN: FROM THE INSIDE OUT, by Feminist Radio Network, n.d. cassette or reel-to-reel. (23 min.) Feminist Radio Network.
A portrait of Lee Brown and her poetry. Through her poetry comes her view of her experiences of streetlife, prostitution, confinement, and the emerging of her own positive self-concept.

564 LEGAL ISSUES AND LEGISLATION AFFECTING WOMEN, by Pacifica Tape Library, 1975. cassette or reel-to-reel. (58 min.) Pacifica Tape Library.
Carol Burris, president of Women's Lobby, presents information regarding the status of women in society vis-à-vis legislation that has been passed. She examines sex discrimination, discrepancies in pay scales, the role of married women in the workplace, and the differing tax rate for women.

565 LESBIAN SEPARATION, by Pacifica Tape Library, 1975. cassette and reel-to-reel. (58 min.) Pacifica Tape Library.
Jan Crawford, convener of the Feminist Community Coalition, Carol Hardin and Doris London, of Lesbian Feminist Liberation, discuss their ideas on lesbian separation.

566 LETTERS FROM A WOMEN HOMESTEADER, by Pacifica Tape Library, n.d. Cassette or reel-to-reel. (26 min.) Pacifica Tape Library.
A dramatization of the diary of Elinore Pruitt Stuart, who homesteaded in Wyoming in 1907.

567 LIBERATION: IS SOCIALISM THE ANSWER?, by Everett/Edwards, Inc., n.d. cassette. Everett/Edwards, Inc.
Narration by Bernice Rosenthal.

568 THE LIFE OF ANNE BRADSTREET, by Everett/Edwards, Inc., n.d. cassette. Everett/Edwards, Inc.
A narration by Hennig Cohen on the life and work of the early American author, Anne Bradstreet.

569 Lord, Audre. [SELECTIONS], by Pacifica Tape Library, 1972. cassette or reel-to-reel. (23 min.) Pacifica Tape Library.
Audre Lord, black woman, poet, mother and teacher reads from her work.

570 MABEL VERNON: SUFFRAGIST, by Melanie Moholick, n.d. cassette or reel-to-reel. (43 min.) Feminist Radio Network.
Mabel Vernon (1883-1975) began organizing in 1913 with the National Women's Party for suffrage. In this interview she talks about the days of marches, pickets, and general disruptions by women rallying around the vote issue.

571 MARGE PIERCY READS HER WORK, by Everett/Edwards, Inc., n.d. cassette. Everett/Edwards, Inc.
The poetry of Marge Piercy read by the author.

572 MARGIE ADAM, by Feminist Radio Network, n.d. cassette or reel-to-reel. (28 min.) Feminist Radio Network.
In an interview with music, Margie discusses her music, the growth of women's culture, and her recent album, Margie Adam, Songwriter.

573 MARILYN HACKER, by Feminist Radio Network, n.d. cassette or reel-to-reel. (29 min.) Feminist Radio Network.
Marilyn Hacker, poet, talks about her life and work and the development of women's poetry from Emily Dickinson to Elizabeth Barrett Browning to Marianne Moore and H.D. (Hilda Doolittle).

574 MARY RICHARDSON WALKER DIARY, by Pacifica Tape Library, n.d. cassette or reel-to-reel. (30 min.) Pacifica Tape Library.
A description of the difficult life of the pioneer woman in America. Mary Richardson Walker was one of the first white women to move west.

Recordings/Spoken Word

575 ME JANE, YOU TARZAN, by Pacifica Tape Library, 1972. cassette or reel-to-reel. (35 min.) Pacifica Tape Library.
A woman archaeologist, Elaine Morgan, questions the interpretations of male archaeologists. She emphasizes the role of she-apes in human development.

576 MENSES, by Feminist Radio Network, n.d. cassette or reel-to-reel. (29 min.) Feminist Radio Network.
A cultural history that explores attitudes towards menstruation through interviews with young girls, African initiation rites, and readings, including The Diary of Anne Frank.

577 MIDWIFERY: PAST AND PRESENT, by Pacifica Tape Library, 1976. cassette and reel-to-reel. (63 min.) Pacifica Tape Library.
A discussion with three midwives of the New York metropolitan area. They discuss the tradition and nature of their work, and why it has been seen as a threat by obstetricians.

578 MISOGYNY IN LITERATURE, by Everett/Edwards, Inc., n.d. cassette. Everett/Edwards, Inc.
Narration by Katherine Rogers.

579 Morgan, Robin. [POEMS], by Pacifica Tape Library, 1972. cassette and reel-to-reel. (37 min.) Pacifica Tape Library.
Robin Morgan reads her poems that portray her feminist views. She expresses her rage at a system man created and the pain of being a woman.

580 MOTORCYCLE WOMEN, by Pacifica Tape Library, 1976. cassette and reel-to-reel. (51 min.) Pacifica Tape Library.
An interview with Dorothy Crouch and Linda Farin, motorcycle activists and publishers of New York's first Motorcycle Woman Newsletter.

581 THE NEGRO WOMAN, by Folkways, n.d. phonorecord. Rounder Records.

582 NO COWARD SOUL: A PORTRAIT OF THE BRONTËS, by Miller Brody, 1973. cassette. Miller Brody.
Margaret Webster reads selections from the stories and poems of the Brontës. Excerpts from letters, diaries, and biographies are also included.
Review: Listening Post, March 1976, p41 ("We get no rounded biographical sketch, but an impressionistic melange ... would interest mainly those who already know the outlines of the Brontës' lives"--Ethel Olicker).

583 NO EASY DECISION, by Aimee Sands, n.d. cassette or reel-to-reel. (25 min.) Feminist Radio Network.
Seven women discuss how they chose to handle unplanned pregnancies. Their stories cover abortion, giving the baby up for adoption, and keeping the baby.

584 O'Connor, Flannery. THE VIOLENT BEAR IT AWAY, n.d. cassette. Everett/Edwards, Inc.
An analysis by Margaret O'Connor of her daughter's story "The Violent Bear It Away."

585 THE OLDER WOMAN, by Pacifica Tape Library, 1976. cassette or reel-to-reel. (112 min.) Pacifica Tape Library.
The financial, political, and emotional problems experienced by older women in our society are considered. Personal accounts from a Conference on the Older Woman.

586 ON GETTING ANGRY, by Pacifica Tape Library, 1972. cassette or reel-to-reel. (64 min.) Pacifica Tape Library.
Many women never learn to express their anger. Six women examine tactics which keep women repressed and depressed, and explore alternatives for constructive expression of anger.

587 OPEN MARRIAGE, by Everett/Edwards, Inc., n.d. cassette. Everett/Edwards, Inc.
Narration by Warren Mintz.

588 Parker, Pat, and Judy Gahn. WHERE WOULD I BE WITHOUT YOU: THE POETRY OF..., by Olivia Records, n.d. phonorecord. Olivia Records.
Pat Parker and Judy Gahn are two San Francisco Bay Area poets. Each woman reads a selection from her work.

589 PEOPLE PAST AND PRESENT: ELLEN TERRY, by Argo Records, n.d. phonorecord. Argo Records.
A dramatized audio biography of Ellen Terry read by Sybil Thorndike.
Reviews: *Listening Post*, September 1975, p24 ("of interest to students of theatre, of women's studies, and of British social history"--Ethel Olicker). *New Records*, April 1975.

590 PEOPLE PAST AND PRESENT: JANE AUSTEN, by Argo records, n.d. phonorecord. Argo Records.
Selections include observations by Charlotte Brontë, Elizabeth Barrett Browning and Virginia Woolf. Literary excerpts are taken from such Austen classics as *Pride and Prejudice* and *Emma*.

Review: <u>Stereo Review</u>, November 1973, p108 ("Lively, diverting, and superbly researched"--Paul Kresh).

591 PETTICOAT POLITICS, by Pacifica Tape Library, 1962. cassette or reel-to-reel. (50 min.) Pacific Tape Library.
A dramatization of the history of women's rights from the abolition movement to the victory of the suffragists.

592 PIONEER WOMEN: SELECTIONS FROM THEIR JOURNALS, by Caedmon Records, n.d. phonorecord or cassette. Caedmon Records.
Selections from the journals of four pioneer women, Elenore Plaisted, Mary Richardson Walker, Martha Summerhays, and Elinor Pruitt Stewart.
Reviews: <u>Listening Post</u>, July 1975, pp24-25 ("The readings ... effectively bring to life the true experiences of these women around the turn of the century"). <u>Booklist</u>, October 1, 1975, p258.

593 Plath, Sylvia. PLATH READS PLATH, by Credo Records, 1975. phonorecord. Bro-Dart.
The readings by the poet of selections from <u>Ariel</u>, <u>Winter Trees</u> and <u>Collected Poems</u> was recorded in 1962. An interview of Sylvia Plath by Peter Orr of the British Council is also included.
Review: <u>Listening Post</u>, Januart 1976, p33 ("It is informative to hear the inflections of a poet reading his or her poetry--specially a poet as subjectively oriented as Sylvia Plath.... Literature and biography mingle and inform each other"--Dennis Petticoffer).

594 THE PLIGHT OF WOMEN IN BROADCASTING, by Pacifica Tape Library, 1972. cassette or reel-to-reel. (71 min.) Pacifica Tape Library.
Three women interview executives from nine San Francisco Bay Area radio and TV stations with interesting results.

595 THE POETRY OF EMILY DICKINSON, by Everett/Edwards, Inc., n.d. cassette. Everett/Edwards, Inc.
Two cassettes of the poetry of Emily Dickinson read by Charles R. Anderson.

596 THE POETRY OF LOUISE BOGAN, by Everett/Edwards, Inc., n.d. cassette. Everett/Edwards, Inc.
The poetry of Louise Bogan read by Paul Ramsey.

597 THE POETRY OF MARIANNE MOORE, by Everett/Edwards, Inc., n.d. Everett/Edwards, Inc.
The poetry of Marianne Moore is discussed by Bernard F. Engel.

598 THE POETRY OF SYLVIA PLATH, by Everett/Edwards, Inc., n.d. Everett/Edwards, Inc.
Discussion by Robert W. Hill.

599 POLLYANNA AND PARLOR DARWINISM, by Pacifica Tape Library, 1975. cassette or reel-to-reel. (58 min.) Pacifica Tape Library.
Cynthia Wolf, associate professor of English, focuses on United States literature during America's period of disunity between the Civil War and World War I, when prepubescent heroines emerged as a symbol of confident innocence. She comments on roles assigned boy and girl characters in the literature.

600 Porche, Veranda. [POEMS], by Pacifica Tape Library, 1972. cassette or reel-to-reel. (35 min.) Pacifica Tape Library.
Veranda Porche reads her poetry, written during her travels throughout the United States which ended on a farm in Vermont.

601 Porter, Katherine Anne. SHIP OF FOOLS, by Everett/Edwards, Inc., n.d. cassette. Everett/Edwards, Inc.
The novel Ship of Fools by Katherine Porter is discussed by Leo Courko.

602 POWER RELATIONS IN THE FAMILY, by Everett/Edwards, Inc., n.d. cassette. Everett/Edwards, Inc.
Narration by Natalie Shainess.

603 THE PREJUDICE OF PARENTS, by Everett/Edwards, Inc., n.d. cassette. Everett/Edwards, Inc.
Narration by Ellen Mintz.

604 PROMISE HER ANYTHING, by Pacifica Tape Library, 1972. cassette or reel-to-reel. (71 min.) Pacifica Tape Library.
An analysis of the cosmetic industry including interviews with marketing executives and advertising executives. Also includes comments by beauty editors of women's magazines, former models, and members of Consumer Action Now.

605 PROSTITUTION, by Red Tape, n.d. cassette or reel-to-reel. (28 min.) Feminist Radio Network.
A documentary in collage form utilizing radio drama, music, and interviews with prostitutes, police officers, and a judge.

606 PROSTITUTION AND THE LAW, by Pacifica Tape Li-

brary, 1976. cassette or reel-to-reel. (52 min.) Pacifica Tape Library.
Among the many facets of the subject explored in this discussion are the paradox of prostitution vis-à-vis feminism, the many myths about prostitution, and immorality in police methods of enforcing vice laws.

607 THE PSYCHOLOGY OF WOMEN, by Everett/Edwards, Inc., n.d. cassette. Everett/Edwards, Inc.
Narration by Florence Denmark.

608 RESTORING WOMEN'S VOICES TO PLANNING, by Everett/Edwards, Inc., n.d. cassette. Everett/Edwards, Inc.
Narration by Margaret Mead.

609 THE REVOLT OF MOTHER, by University of California Extension Media, 1974. cassette. (30 min.) University of California Extension Media Center.
Based on a story by Mary Wilkins Freeman written in 1891 about a woman's revolt against oppression.
Review: Booklist, September 15, 1976, p198 ("This dramatic narrative gives a feeling of the oppression American women faced in the nineteenth century as well as reflects their courage").

610 Rich, Adrienne, et al. A SIGN/I WAS NOT ALONE, by Out and Out Records, n.d. phonorecord. Ladyslipper Music.
Readings of the poets Adrienne Rich, Honor Moore, Audre Lord, and Joan Larkin.

611 THE ROLE OF WOMEN IN THE ARTS, by Pacifica Tape Library, n.d. cassette or reel-to-reel. (63 min.) Pacifica Tape Library.
A discussion about the problems facing women in the arts with art critic John Perreault and others: Cindy Nemser, Deborah Remington, Sylvia Sleigh, and Brenda Miller.

612 ROLE PLAYING, by Pacifica Tape Library, 1972. cassette or reel-to-reel. (59 min.) Pacifica Tape Library.
Six women discuss society's equation of marriage, motherhood, and heterosexuality with "success"; political, sexual, and personal implications of lesbianism; and abortion and celibacy.

613 ROMAINE BROOKS, by Feminist Radio Network, n.d. cassette or reel-to-reel. (32 min.) Feminist Radio Network.
The life and work of artist Romaine Brooks is

discussed by Anne Imelda Radiu, art historian and curator of the National Gallery of Art.

614 A ROOM OF ONE'S OWN, PART I AND II, by Feminist Radio Network, n.d. 2 cassettes or reel-to-reel. (29 min. each) Feminist Radio Network.
Actress Jane Batt reads from speeches and essays of Virginia Woolf. The topics range from conditions of women in her era, to androgyny, to creative writing.

615 SADIE AND MAUDE, by Pacifica Tape Library, 1971. cassette or reel-to-reel. (36 min.) Pacifica Tape Library.
Jeanette Henderson and Linda Taylor read black women's poetry and discuss black vs. women's liberation.

616 Sanchez, Sonia. A SUN LADY FOR ALL SEASONS READS HER POETRY, by Folkways Records, n.d. Folkways Records.
Sanchez, a black, reads some of her work.
Review: Booklist, June 1, 1974, p1095 ("For ... those with an interest in the new black poetry which abounds at the moment").

617 A SECRETARY IS NOT A TOY: OFFICE WORKERS, by Red Tape, n.d. cassette or reel-to-reel. (29 min.) Feminist Radio Network.
Here, "the girls" in the office talk about low pay, job discrimination, the lack of respect for them as skilled professionals, and the need for unionization.

618 SEDUCED AND ABANDONED IN AMERICAN LITERATURE, by Everett/Edwards, Inc., n.d. cassette. Everett/Edwards, Inc.
Narration by Wendy Martine.

619 SEX AND DIVORCE, by Pacifica Tape Library, 1972. cassette or reel-to-reel. (46 min.) Pacifica Tape Library.
This group centers on sexual problems, role conditioning and isolation in marriage. Participants discuss their decisions and efforts to change their lives and roles.

620 SEXISM, by YWCA of Canada, 1975. cassette. (90 min.) YWCA of Canada.
A three-part discussion about sexism. Part I is an overview of sexism and information on research that has been undertaken. Part 2 is a discussion of how sexism affects people in a personal sense. Part 3 examines the implications of sexism for programs of local associations.

621 Sexton, Anne. ANNE SEXTON READS HER POETRY, by Caedmon Records, n.d. phonorecord. Caedmon Records.

93   Recordings/Spoken Word

A selection of Sexton's poetry read by the poet.

622 SIDE BY SIDE, RE-ENACTMENTS OF SCENES FROM WOMEN'S HISTORY, 1848-1920. phonorecord. Galaxia Women Enterprises.

A two-phonorecord set which chronicles the early feminist activity with a collection of speeches delivered by the leaders of the movement woven into the fabric of a thoroughly researched historical narrative. Some of the women heard are Lucretia Mott, Susan B. Anthony, Elizabeth Cady Stanton and Sojourner Truth.

623 SINFUL EVE, by University of California Extension Media Center, 1974. cassette. (29 min.) University of California Extension Media Center.

Examines the beginning of the repudiation of the theory that woman, through Eve, is responsible for the sinfulness of humankind.

Review: Booklist, September 15, 1976, p198 ("valuable ... for those seeking an understanding of the Puritan view of woman and the roots of women's present status").

624 THE SINGER AS AN ACTIVIST, n.d. cassette. Women's Audio Exchange.

Joan Baez discusses her music and politics.

625 THE SINGLE WOMAN, by Pacifica Tape Library, 1972. cassette or reel-to-reel. (47 min.) Pacifica Tape Library.

Six women relate their personal experiences in marriage and discuss dating, engagement, infidelity, the fear of being single, divorce, and the ultimate realization that marriage is not a short cut to fulfillment.

626 SISTERS BY CHOICE, by Pacifica Tape Library, 1975. cassette and reel-to-reel. (50 min.) Pacifica Tape Library.

An interview with the musical group, Sisters by Choice. They discuss their work and play some examples which attempt to debunk the old standard myths about the role of women in our society.

627 SOCIAL IMAGES OF WOMEN IN FILM, by Everett/Edwards, Inc., n.d. cassette. Everett/Edwards, Inc.
Narration by Natalie Shainess.

628 SOCIAL ROLES IN AMERICA, by Everett/Edwards Inc., n.d. cassette. Everett/Edwards, Inc.
Narration by Sheila Tobias.

629 SPEAK OUT: POOR WOMEN IN THE ECONOMY, by Feminist Radio Network, n.d. cassette or reel-to-reel. (60 min.) Feminist Radio Network.

Women's Nonprint Media   94

A documentary based on a Congressional hearing organized by the National Committee on Household Employees. Shirley Chisholm opens the speakouts in which women tell in their own words what it's like to be poor, female and without resources.

630 Stowe, Harriet Beecher. UNCLE TOM'S CABIN, by Everett/Edwards, Inc. n.d. cassette. Everett/Edwards, Inc.
The famous 19th-century novel is discussed by Helen Jaskoski.

631 SUSAN BROWNMILLER: AGAINST OUR WILL, by Pacifica Tape Library, 1976. cassette or reel-to-reel. (77 min.) Pacifica Tape Library.
A recording of Susan Brownmiller's lecture at Keene State College. She presents a thesis that sexual force is used to keep women in their inferior position.

632 SUSAN BROWNMILLER ON WRITING AND PROMOTING, by Pacifica Tape Library, 1976. cassette or reel-to-reel. (63 min.) Pacifica Tape Library.
An interview with Brownmiller, author of the book Against Our Will--Men, Women and Rape. She felt her mission in the feminist movement, after hearing women speaking openly about their rapes, was to compile the history of rape in a sound and rational analysis.

633 SWEET HONEY IN THE ROCK "BELIEVE I'LL RUN ON...," by Feminist Radio Network, n.d. cassette or reel-to-reel. (28 min.) Feminist Radio Network.
Interviewed just after the release of their album, "Believe I'll Run On... See What the End's Gonna Be," the a cappella singing group talks about the roots and traditions of their music and the meaning of their group, their goals and their songs.

634 Swenson, May. THE POETRY AND VOICE OF..., by Caedmon Records, n.d. phonorecord. Caedmon Records.
From a poetry reading at the Poetry Center in New York. Swenson reads her poetry and discusses its patterns and objectives.
Review: Previews, January 1977, p30 ("will be of great interest in extending the listener's acquaintance with this highly respected poet"--Margaret Bush).

635 Tomlin, Lily. MODERN SCREAM, 1975. phonorecord. Polydor Records.
Selections include "Exclusive Interview," "Rubber Freak," Suzie Sorority," Adult Sex Education," "Judith Beasley Exclusive," "Dear Dr. Dacey," "The Trip," and others.
Review: Listening Post, January 1976, p34 ("an effort to satirize the side of the female experience that

perpetuates movie magazines, the intent is a bit too tinged with venom and the humor too flat to lift it much above desperation"--Sheldon Bull).

636 TRAINING THE WOMAN TO KNOW HER PLACE, by Pacifica Tape Library, 1971. cassette or reel-to-reel. (60 min.) Pacifica Tape Library.
With the use of role playing games, psychologists Darryl and Sandra Bem demonstrate that social conditioning is responsible for the lack of motivation among women to pursue other than normal careers.

637 VOICES FROM WITHIN, by Pacifica Tape Library, 1975. cassette or reel-to-reel. (40 min.) Pacifica Tape Library.
Several women prisoners serving long-term sentences at the New York State Correctional Facility discuss "doing time" and their hopes for change within the system.

638 WAS JESUS A FEMINIST?, by Everett/Edwards, Inc., n.d. cassette. Everett/Edwards, Inc.
Narration by Michael Southwell.

639 Welty, Eudora. LOSING BATTLES, by Everett/Edwards, Inc., n.d. cassette. Everett/Edwards, Inc.
Her recent novel is commented on by Robert Griffin.

640 Wharton, Edith. THE AGE OF INNOCENCE, by Everett/Edwards, Inc., n.d. cassette. Everett/Edwards.
The famous novel is discussed by J.W. Tuttleton.

641 WHAT'S NORMAL: AN EXPLORATION OF HOMOSEXUALITY AND THE GAY SUBCULTURE IN OUR SOCIETY, by Frieda Werden and Stewart Wilber, 1976. 13 cassette or reel-to-reel tapes. (25 min. each) KUT-FM.
The various programs are entitled: (1) Homosexuality in Cultural Content, (2) The Psychological Establishment and the Gay Client, (3) Gay Rights and the Legal Status of Homosexuals, (4) Parents and Gay Children, (5) The Homophile in Literature, (6) The Motivations and Means of Gay Activism, (7) The Lesbian Separatists, (8) Racism and the Gay Community, (9) Gay Men's Movement, (10) Grass-Roots Gay Counseling, (11) Bisexuality: A Door That Swings Both Ways, (12) Gays and Role Playing, (13) Gay Bar Scene.

642 WHO IS A VIOLENT WOMAN?, by Aimee Sands, n.d. cassette or reel-to-reel. (30 min.) Feminist Radio Network.
This program explores the concept of violence in women and the circumstances of women hospitalized and incarcerated for violent behavior. New approaches to treating violence in women and society are also discussed.

643 WOMAN--GLIMPSES OF PORTRAITS FROM SHAKE-SPEARE'S GALLERY OF WOMEN, by Folkways Records, n.d. phonorecord. Folkways Records.
Women as portrayed in Shakespeare: a concert reading performed by Claire Luce in 1964.

644 A WOMAN SPEAKS, by University of California Extension Media Center, 1974. cassette. (29 min.) University of California Extension Media Center.
Recounts the events leading to the banishment and excommunication of Anne Hutchinson from the Massachusetts Bay Colony.
Review: Booklist, September 15, 1976, p198 ("examines the Puritan emphasis on obedience, especially for women. Using period expressions ... gives the listener the feeling of colonial attitudes.... Of interest to ... consciousness raising women").

645 WOMEN ALONE, by Pacifica Tape Libary, 1976. cassette or reel-to-reel. (58 min.) Pacifica Tape Library.
Discusses the changes in identity women experience after divorce, separation or death of a husband, why our society is so "couple-oriented," the attitudes toward widowed or single women, and how the women's movement helps women that are alone.

646 WOMEN AND BREAST CANCER, by Pacifica Tape Library, 1976. cassette or reel-to-reel. (40 min.) Pacifica Tape Library.
Rose Kushner, author of Breast Cancer: A Personal history and an Investigative Report, presents her findings on the 15 different kinds of breast cancer and a history of her own experience from discovery of a suspicious lump through a mastectomy operation.

647 WOMEN AND COUNTRY MUSIC, PART I AND II, by Sophie's Parlor, n.d. 2 cassettes or reel-to-reel (59 min. each) Feminist Radio Network.
Traces the role women have played in the growth of country music. Part I covers the traditional heritage, Part II features the history of female country singers recorded in Nashville from 1950 to the present.

648 WOMEN AND EMPLOYMENT, by Everett/Edwards, Inc., n.d. cassette. Everett/Edwards, Inc.
Narration by Leo Kanowitz.

649 WOMEN AND MENTAL HEALTH, by Pacifica Tape Library, 1975. cassette or reel-to-reel. (55 min.) Pacifica Tape Library.
Discussion of the impact of social and cultural restrictions on women and other minorities, and their con-

Recordings/Spoken Word

nection to insanity. Links the high incidence of women undergoing psychiatric treatment to the limiting roles women are expected to assume in our society.

650 WOMEN AND THE LAW, by Everett/Edwards, Inc., n.d. cassette. Everett/Edwards, Inc.
Narration by Leo Kanowitz.

651 WOMEN AS A MINORITY GROUP, by Everett/Edwards, Inc., n.d. cassette. Everett/Edwards, Inc.
Narration by Helen Hacker.

652 WOMEN AS LITERARY INNOVATORS, by Everett/Edwards, Inc., n.d. cassette. Everett/Edwards, Inc.
Narration by Grace Shulman.

653 WOMAN AS SUBJECT AND OBJECT IN LITERATURE, by Everett/Edwards, Inc., n.d. cassette. Everett/Edwards, Inc.
Narration by Barbara Lovenheim.

654 WOMEN, CULTURE, AND SOCIETY, by Pacifica Tape Library, 1975. cassette or reel-to-reel. (56 min.) Pacifica Tape Library.
An historical examination of the development of women's societal role. Examples are given of past societies in which women were more productive and played a far more active role than in our own.

655 WOMEN IN ADVERTISING, by Pacifica Tape Library, 1973. cassette or reel-to-reel. (48 min.) Pacifica Tape Library.
Conversation among an ad executive and Jane Trahey, Ann Tolstoy and Pat Carbine about the image of women portrayed by the media.

656 WOMAN IN ANCIENT ROME, by Everett/Edwards, Inc., n.d. Everett/Edwards, Inc.
Narration by Daniel Coogan.

657 WOMEN IN ANTIQUITY, by Pacifica Tape Library, 1976. cassette or reel-to-reel. (51 min.) Pacifica Tape library.
Professor Sarah Pomeroy, author of Goddesses, Whores, Wives and Slaves, describes and comments on the life and times of women in ancient Greece and Rome.

658 WOMEN IN ART, by Pacifica Tape Library, 1971. cassette or reel-to-reel. (63 min.) Pacifica Tape Library.
Successful women artists discuss their problems, frustrations, and rewards. Participants include Lucy Lip-

pard, Cindy Nemser, Ruth Nodicka, Cece Roser, and others.

659 WOMEN IN BANGLADESH, by Everett/Edwards, Inc., n.d. cassette. Everett/Edwards, Inc.
Narration by Shirley Lindenbaum.

660 WOMEN IN CHILE, by Pacifica Tape Library, 1975. cassette or reel-to-reel. (63 min.) Pacifica Tape Library.
Discusses the conditions which led to the overthrow of the Allende government and describes the large roles played by upper class Chilean women.

661 WOMEN IN CHINA, by Everett/Edwards, Inc. n.d. cassette. Everett/Edwards, Inc.
Narration by Sari Knopp Bicklen.

662 WOMEN IN DOSTOYEVSKY, by Everett/Edwards, Inc., n.d. cassette. Everett/Edwards, Inc.
Narration by Deborah Fort.

663 WOMEN IN EARLY AMERICAN LITERATURE, by Everett/Edwards, Inc., n.d. cassette. Everett/Edwards, Inc.
A discussion of women poets and writers in early American literature by Kay S. House.

664 WOMEN IN FAULKNER, by Everett/Edwards, Inc., n.d. cassette. Everett/Edwards, Inc.
Narration by Martha Nochimson.

665 WOMEN IN FRANCE, by Everett/Edwards, Inc., n.d. cassette. Everett/Edwards, Inc.
Narration by Anna Raitiere.

666 WOMEN IN INDIA, by Pacifica Tape Library, 1976. cassette or reel-to-reel. (60 min.) Pacifica Tape Library.
In delineating the various origins and forms of oppression under which Indian women live, the interview with Laura Shapiro, a feminist journalist, presents insights into many religious/cultural aspects of India.

667 WOMEN IN LATIN AMERICA by Everett/Edwards, Inc., n.d cassette. Everett/Edwards, Inc.
Narration by Gloria Waldman.

668 WOMEN IN MANAGEMENT, by Educational Communications, 1973. 6 cassettes. (30 min. each) Mainstream International.
Employs dramatization to help women learn about

working demands of management roles. Examines the identification and development of leadership potential.
Review: <u>Booklist</u>, July 15, 1975, p1182 ("A comprehensive new program for developing managerial talent among women employees").

669 WOMEN IN MEDIA, by Pacifica Tape Library, 1970. cassette or reel-to-reel. (61 min.) Pacifica Tape Library.
Nicholas Johnson speaks before the American Women in Radio and Television about some of the things the network would rather not have women know about.

670 WOMEN IN MEDIEVAL LITERATURE, by Everett/Edwards, Inc., n.d. cassette. Everett/Edwards, Inc.
Narration by Joan Ferrante.

671 WOMEN IN MILTON, PART I AND PART 2, by Everett/Edwards, Inc., n.d. 2 cassettes. Everett/Edwards, Inc.
Narration by Joan Hartman.

672 WOMEN IN MODERN JEWISH AMERICAN FICTION, by Everett/Edwards, Inc., n.d. cassette. Everett/Edwards, Inc.
Narration by Charles Shapiro.

673 WOMEN IN SHAKESPEARE: CLASSICAL FIGURES, by Everett/Edwards, Inc., n.d. cassette. Everett/Edwards, Inc.
Narration by Margaret Ranald.

674 WOMEN IN SHAKESPEARE'S COMEDIES, by Everett/Edwards, Inc., n.d. cassette. Everett/Edwards, Inc.
Narration by Margaret Ranald.

675 WOMEN IN SHAKESPEARE'S HISTORIES, by Everett/Edwards, Inc., n.d. cassette. Everett/Edwards, Inc.
Narration by Margaret Ranald.

676 WOMEN IN SHAKESPEARE'S LAST PLAYS, by Everett/Edwards, Inc., n.d. cassette. Everett/Edwards, Inc.
Narration by Margaret Ranald.

677 WOMEN IN SHAKESPEARE'S TRAGEDIES, by Everett/Edwards, Inc., n.d. cassette. Everett/Edwards, Inc.
Narration by Margaret Ranald.

Women's Nonprint Media   100

678 WOMEN IN SICILY, by Everett/Edwards, Inc., n.d. cassette. Everett/Edwards, Inc.
Narration by Jane Schneider.

679 WOMEN IN SPARTA AND ATHENS, by Everett/Edwards, Inc., n.d. Everett/Edwards, Inc.
Narration by Sarah Pomeroy.

680 WOMEN IN THE AMERICAN WEST, by Everett/Edwards, Inc., n.d. cassette. Everett/Edwards, Inc.
Narration by T.A. Larson.

681 WOMEN IN THE ARTS, by Pacifica Tape Library, 1971. cassette or reel-to-reel. (29 min.) Pacifica Tape Library.
Anais Nin and Judy Chicago talk about the history of female consciousness in art.

682 WOMEN IN THE BRONZE AGE OF GREECE, by Everett/Edwards, Inc., n.d. cassette. Everett/Edwards.
Narration by Sarah Pomeroy.

683 WOMEN IN THE JUDAIC-CHRISTIAN TRADITION, by Pacifica Tape Library, 1975. cassette or reel-to-reel. (58 min.) Pacifica Tape Library.
A talk on women in religious history. Explores myths portraying women as either "dehumanized or super-humanized." Contrasts women's roles in the two religions and explores how they have altered them.

684 WOMEN IN THE MODERN NOVEL, by Everett/Edwards, Inc., n.d. cassette. Everett/Edwards, Inc.
Narration by Katherine Henderson.

685 WOMEN IN YEATS AND ELIOT, by Everett/Edwards, Inc., n.d. cassette. Everett/Edwards, Inc.
Narration by Carol Smith.

686 WOMEN OF THE PRESS: HARRIET VAN HORNE, by Pacifica Tape Library, 1971. cassette or reel-to-reel. (22 min.) Pacifica Tape Library.
The New York Post columnist describes being a successful woman of the press, giving views on many issues.

687 WOMEN: THE DANGEROUS SEX, by Everett/Edwards, Inc., n.d. cassette. Everett/Edwards, Inc.
Discussion by H.R. Hays.

688 WOMEN TODAY: OPTIONS, OBSTACLES, OPPORTUNITIES, by Mass Communications, Inc., 1974. 6 cassettes. (40 min. ea.) Mass Communications, Inc.
Interviews important women in today's society.

Includes Margaret Mead, Matina Horner, Caroline Bird, and Elizabeth Janeway.
Review: Previews, December 1975, p37 ("fascinating interviews ... will stimulate the fiber of today's woman's consciousness"--Phyllis Zucker).

689 WOMEN, WITCHES, AND WORSHIP, by Everett/Edwards, Inc., n.d. cassette. Everett/Edwards, Inc.
Narration by Margot Adler.

690 WOMEN'S LIBERATION AND BLACK CIVIL RIGHTS, by Pacifica Tape Library, 1972. cassette or reel-to-reel. (72 min.) Pacifica Tape Library.
A talk by Catherine Stimpson on the tensions between black women and feminists. It is followed by a question and answer period in which several well-known feminists state their disagreements with the speaker.

691 WOMEN'S LIBERATION AND THE ARTS, by Pacifica Tape Library, 1971. cassette or reel-to-reel. (66 min.) Pacifica Tape Library.
Kate Millett, Louise Nevelson, Grace Paley and others in a panel discussion on the effects of liberation on women.

692 WOMEN'S LIBERATION AND THE NEW MYTHS OF MOTHERHOOD, by Lansford Publishing Company, 1976. 2 cassettes. (50 min. each) Lansford Publishing Company.
Narrated and written by Shirley Radl, author of Mother's Day Is Over.

693 WOMEN'S LIBERATION IN CHINA, by Pacifica Tape Library, 1975. cassette or reel-to-reel. (60 min.) Pacifica Tape Library.
Diane Feeley lectures on the struggle of Chinese women for liberation from their traditional subservient roles. She traces the history of women's labor unions and self-defense groups, and the effects of the 1949 Cultural Revolution on ending such barbaric practices as slavery, foot-binding and child brides.

694 WOMEN'S ORGASMS: FACT, FANTASY OR PHALLACY? by Dale Davidson, n.d. cassette or reel-to-reel. (29 min.) Feminist Radio Network.
A discussion on the myths, taboos and misinformation associated with the subject of female sexuality from the Freudian and Kinsey views to the so-called sexual revolution of the 60's.

695 WOMEN'S ROLES IN SOCIETY, by Educational Records, n.d. phonorecord. Educational Records.

A discussion of the emerging debate over women's role in the modern world, including cultural expectations, stereotypic notions, and access to school and job opportunities.

696 THE WOMEN'S SUFFRAGIST MOVEMENT, by Pacifica Tape Library, 1976. cassette or reel-to-reel. (51 min.) Pacifica Tape Library.
Susan Remny uses the historical approach and the examples of Susan B. Anthony, Elizabeth Cady Stanton, and others to analyze the present women's movement.

697 Woolf, Virginia. THE LETTERS OF..., by Cinema/Sound Ltd., 1976. cassette. (55 min.) Jeffrey Norton Publishers.
The letters of Virginia Woolf are used to provide a portrait of the author. Editor Nigel Nicolson recalls her brilliance.

698 THE WORK OF THE WOMEN, by Activity Records, 1976. phonorecord or cassette. (34 min.) Educational Activities.
Explores the feelings of women in story and song from the Revolution to the present.

699 THE WORKS OF DENISE LEVERTOV, by Everett/Edwards, Inc., n.d. cassette. Everett/Edwards, Inc.
Discussion by Charles Molesworth.

700 THE WORKS OF DORIS LESSING, by Everett/Edwards, Inc., n.d. cassette. Everett/Edwards, Inc.
Lecture by Virginia Tiger.

701 THE WORKS OF ELLEN GLASGOW, by Everett/Edwards, Inc., n.d. cassette. Everett/Edwards, Inc.
C. Hugh Holman discusses the works of Ellen Glasgow.

702 THE WORKS OF EUDORA WELTY, by Everett/Edwards, Inc., n.d. cassette. Everett/Edwards, Inc.
Comment by Ruth Vande Kieft.

703 THE WORKS OF FLANNERY O'CONNOR, by Everett/Edwards, Inc., n.d. cassette. Everett/Edwards, Inc.
A discussion of O'Connor's works by Carter Martin.

704 THE WORKS OF FLANNERY O'CONNOR, by Everett/Edwards, Inc., n.d. cassette. Everett/Edwards, Inc.
Discussion by Preston M. Browning, Jr.

Recordings/Spoken Word

705 THE WORKS OF GERTRUDE STEIN, by Everett/Edwards, Inc., n.d. cassette. Everett/Edwards, Inc.
    Discussion by Constance Ayers Denne.

706 THE WORKS OF JOYCE CAROL OATES, by Everett/Edwards, Inc., n.d. cassette. Everett/Edwards, Inc.
    Lecture by Constance Ayers Denne.

707 THE WORKS OF KATE CHOPIN, by Everett Edwards, Inc., n.d. cassette. Everett/Edwards, Inc.
    Readings from the work of Kate Chopin by C. Hugh Holman and a critique of the work.

708 THE WORKS OF LILLIAN HELLMAN, by Everett/Edwards, Inc., n.d. cassette. Everett/Edwards, Inc.
    A discussion of the work of Lillian Hellman by Kimball King.

709 THE WORKS OF MARY AUSTON, by Everett/Edwards, Inc., n.d. cassette. Everett/Edwards, Inc.
    Selections of the author's works read by Jo Lyday with a discussion of the literature.

710 THE WORKS OF PHILLIS WHEATLEY, by Everett/Edwards, Inc., n.d. cassette. Everett/Edwards, Inc.
    Discussion by Houston A. Baker, Jr.

711 THE WORKS OF SARAH ORNE JEWETT, by Everett/Edwards, Inc., n.d. cassette. Everett/Edwards, Inc.
    Discussion by William Randell.

712 THE WORKS OF SYLVIA PLATH, by Everett/Edwards, Inc., n.d. cassette. Everett/Edwards, Inc.
    Discussion by Evelyn Greenberger.

713 YOUNG AND FEMALE, by Women's Audio Exchange, n.d. phonorecord/cassette. Women's Audio Exchange.
    Selections from the biographies of Margaret Sanger, Margaret Bourke-White, Shirley Chisholm, Dorothy Day, Shirley MacLaine, Emily Hahn. Performance by Sandy Dennis, Eileen Heckart and Claudia McNeil.

714 YOUNG AND FEMALE, by Educational Records, n.d. phonorecord. Educational Records.
    Interviews with women who have been successful in fields normally reserved for men. Some of the participants are Margaret Sanger, Margaret Bourke-White, Shirley Chisholm, and Shirley MacLaine.

RECORDINGS/MUSIC

715 Adam, Margie. MARGIE ADAM, SONGWRITER, by Pleiades Records, n.d. phonorecord/cassette. Pleiades Records.
Recordings of the songs of Margie Adam by the artist.

716 Allen, Indra. LONER, by Indra Allen, 1978. phonorecord. Indra Allen.
Field recordings of the songs and guitar of Indra Allen. Songs of women's experiences, feminism, autonomy.

717 ANY OLD TIME STRING BAND, by Arhoolie, n.d. phonorecord. Rounder Records.
Bluegrass music.

718 Arlington Street Women's Caucus. HONOR THY WOMANSELF: SONGS OF LIBERATION, by the Caucus, n.d. phonorecord. Rounder Records.
This album is a product, not of a singing group, but of a women's group. The music could be described as "uninhibited folk"--a product of what happens when friends come together to make music, feminist music.

719 Arlington Street Women's Caucus. LEAVE THE BREADS A'BURNING, by the Caucus, n.d. phonorecord. Maireen Newell.
Another album of the group described above. Folk feminist music--music relevant to women.

720 Armstrong, Frankie. OUT OF LOVE, HOPE, AND SUFFERING..., by Bay Records, n.d. phonorecord. Bay Records.
Britain's foremost female folksinger, Frankie Armstrong, accompanied by California friends, has compiled her "American" album of her most popular traditional and contemporary songs.

721 Artau, Estrella. ALGO SE QUEMA ALLA AFUERA (Something Is Burning Out There), by Paredon Records, n.d. phonorecord. Paredon Records.

Estrella Artau sings of Puerto Rico, but also of other oppressed peoples in the Caribbean and Latin America.

722 Baba Yaga. ON THE EDGE, by Bloodleaf Records, n.d. phonorecord. Olivia Records.
Baba Yaga is a Portland, Oregon based eight piece women's band. Their instruments are trumpet, sax, flute, congas, piano, bass, guitar, drums, and vocals.

723 BANJO PICKIN' GIRLS, by Rounder Records, n.d. phonorecord. Rounder Records.
Early bluegrass women from old recordings.

724 Be Be K'Roche. BE BE K'ROCHE, by Olivia Records, n.d. phonorecord. Olivia Records.
This San Francisco Bay Area women's band plays a blend of Latin, rhythm and blues, and jazz. Be Be K'Roche members are Virginia Rubino, keyboards and vocals; Jerene O'Brien, electric guitar and vocals; Peggy Mitchell, fender bass and vocals; and Janet Lampert, drums and vocals.

725 Berkeley Women's Music Collective. BERKELEY WOMEN'S MUSIC COLLECTIVE, by The Collective, 1976. phonorecord. Olivia Records.
The Collective consists of Nancy Vogl on acoustic guitar and tenor sax; Debbie Lempke on electric and acoustic guitar, bass; Susann Shanbaum on bass, harmonica, electric and acoustic guitar; Nancy Henderson on piano. All members compose, arrange and sing original material.
Review: Country Women, December 1976, p56 ("excellently documents the pain and struggle of being a woman in this patriarchical society").

726 Berkeley Women's Music Collective. TRYING TO SURVIVE, by Olivia Records, n.d. phonorecord. Olivia Records.
The group's second album features ten original songs. Guitar, piano, bass, drums, and harmonica arrangements have jazz, country, Latin, and rock influences.

727 Bonar, Connie. CONNIE FIDDLES CANADIAN, by American Heritage Records, n.d. phonorecord. Rounder Records.

728 Brake, Marita. THE OTHER SIDE NOW/JAY IN THE MORNING, by Maritamusic, n.d. phonorecord (45 rpm) Maritamusic.

729 BUFFALO GALS, by Revonah Records, n.d. phonorecord. Rounder Records.
Bluegrass music.

730 Carter, Dorothy, and others. TROUBADOUR, n.d. phonorecord. Ladyslipper Music.

Dorothy Carter, Sally Hilmer, and Connie Demby and the sounds of the hammered dulcimer, the psaltery, flute, tamboura and the ch'in.

731 Cazden, Joanna. THE GREATEST ILLUSION, by Sister Sun Records, n.d. phonorecord. Ladyslipper Music.
The first album of Joanna Cazden. Includes feminist and spiritual songs.

732 Cazden, Joanna. HATCHING, by Sister Sun Records, n.d. phonorecord. Olivia Records.
Songs of political action, mystical awakening, and the lives and struggles of women. Joanna performs on guitar, autoharp, and the recorder. She is backed up by bass, piano, fiddle and a chorus of Boston Area women musicians, in styles ranging from soft-jazz to driving folk.

733 Chicago and New Haven Women's Liberation Rock Bands. MOUNTAIN MOVING DAY, by Rounder Records, n.d. phonorecord. Rounder Records.

734 Christian, Meg. FACE THE MUSIC, by Olivia Records, n.d. phonorecord. Olivia Records.
Meg Christian sings women-identified songs, joined by Sweet Honey in the Rock, Mary Watkins, Diane Lindsay, Teresa Trull, Holly Near, among others.

735 Christian, Meg. I KNOW YOU KNOW, by Olivia Records, 1975. phonorecord. Olivia Records.
Christian--songwriter, guitarist, autoharpist--sings "Song to My Mamma," "Ode to a Gym Teacher," etc.
Review: Country Women, December 1976, p56 ("Speaks honestly and realistically to women").

736 Clarke, Rebecca, and Hoover, Katherine. WORKS BY REBECCA CLARKE AND KATHERINE HOOVER, 1974. phonorecord. Leonarda Productions Inc.
The album consists of: "Trio (1921) for violin, cello, and piano" by Rebecca Clarke and "Trio (1978) for violin, cello, and piano" by Katherine Hoover.

737 Clemmens, Ginni. I'M LOOKIN' FOR SOME LONG-TIME FRIENDS, by Open Door Records, n.d. phonorecord. Ladyslipper Music.
Songs played on guitar and sung by Ginni Clemmens. A woman-produced recording.

738 Culver, Casse. CASSE CULVER IN CONCERT, by Hera Audio Productions, 1975. cassette. Sweet Alliance.
Eight songs recorded at a concert at the Los Angeles Women's Building in 1974. Feminist folk music.

Recordings/Music

739 Culver, Casse. THREE GYPSIES, by Urana Records, 1976. phonorecord. Olivia Records.
Casse Culver plays guitar, autoharp, harmonica and sings the lead vocals, drawing selections from the many songs she has written, as well as songs by other women.

740 Dane, Barbara. FTA! SONGS OF THE G.I. RESISTANCE, by Paredon Records, n.d. phonorecord. Paredon Records.
Recorded at G.I. coffee houses and movement centers at Fort Hood, Texas, Fort Benning, Ga., and Fort Bragg, N.C.

741 Dane, Barbara. I HATE THE CAPITALIST SYSTEM, by Paredon Records, n.d. phonorecord. Paredon Records.
Songs of the America working class and the struggle against oppression. Songs of miners, auto workers, migrant workers, and working-class women.

742 DEADLY NIGHTSHADE, by Phantom Records, n.d. phonorecord. Phantom Records.
Contains songs of liberation that feminists and non-feminists can relate to. The music has strong country-western tones.

743 DEBBY McCLATCHY, by Green Lennet Records, n.d. phonorecord. Rounder Records.
Bluegrass music.

744 Dickens, Hazel, and Gerrard, Alice. HAZEL AND ALICE, by Rounder Records, n.d. phonorecord. Ladyslipper Music.
Bluegrass, country and some of their original material. The songs reflect their feminist consciousness and their respect for traditional music.

745 Dickens, Hazel, and Gerrard, Alice. HAZEL AND ALICE: WON'T YOU COME AND SING FOR ME?, by Folkways records, n.d. phonorecord. Rounder Records.
Bluegrass music.

746 Dobkin, Alix. LIVING WITH LESBIANS, by Woman's Wax Works, n.d. phonorecord. Ladyslipper Music.
Original songs of Alix Dobkin and a few traditional Balkan songs.

747 Edell, Therese. FROM WOMEN'S FACES, by Sea Friends Records, 1978. phonorecord. Ladyslipper Music.
This album of pop and folk style music was written mostly by Therese with a couple of songs by Annie Diner-

man. Musicans and production mostly by women. The songs are about women friends, relationships with loves and relatives, and being alone.

748 Etzler, Carole. SOMETIMES I WISH, by Sisters Unlimited, n.d. phonorecord. Sisters Unlimited.
    The album is a musical journal. The songs are all written about personal events in the artist's life.
    Review: Media Report to Women, Mary 1, 1976, p3.

749 Etzler, Carole. WOMENRIVER FLOWING ON, by Sisters Unlimited, n.d. phonorecord. Sisters Unlimited.
    Carole Etzler, voice and guitar, and seven other women in a blend of flute, piano, autoharp, bass and acoustic guitar sings songs about women's feelings.

750 Faithe. ODE TO ANITA, by Jun Mhoone Records, n.d. phonorecord (45 rpm) Ladyslipper Music.
    Two original songs "Ode to Anita" and "Five Years Tonight". One speaks to the absurdity of the Anita Bryant anti-gay campaign.

751 Feldman, Maxine. CLOSET SALE, 1979. phonorecord. Galaxia Women Enterprises.
    An album of all original songs by Maxine Feldman containing powerful political messages.

752 Fire, Kathy. SONGS OF FIRE: SONGS OF A LESBIAN ANARCHIST, by Folkways Records, n.d. phonorecords. Rounder Records.

753 Gardner, Kay. EMERGING, by Wise Women Enterprise, 1978. phonorecord. Ladyslipper Music.
    The sounds range from Renaissance to contemporary. Composed by Kay Gardner and played by her and a host of other classical musicians.

754 Gardner, Kay. MOONCIRCLES. Wise Women Enterprises, Inc., n.d. phonorecord. Olivia Records.
    The music is written, arranged, and performed by Kay Gardner. Kay plays her flutes with other women musicians on guitar, keyboard, strings, and small percussion in five instrumental pieces. She accompanies herself on autoharp or guitar for three songs.
    Review: Country Women, December 1976, p56 ("beautiful flute instrumentals. If there is an album of women's spirituality, this is it!").

755 GIRLS OF THE GOLDEN WEST, by Sonyaton Records, n.d. phonorecord. Rounder Records.
    Bluegrass music.

756 Glanville Hicks, Peggy. NAUSICAA--SCENES FROM THE OPERA, by Ladyslipper Music, n.d. phonorecord. Ladyslipper Music.

757 GOOD OLE PERSONS STRING BAND, by Bay Records, n.d. phonorecord. Rounder Records.
Bluegrass music.

758 Grant, Beverly. WORKING PEOPLE GONNA RISE, by Paredon Records, n.d. phonorecord. Paredon Records.
Beverly Grant is the organizer of the group and the composer of most of its songs. She has a long history of identification with the women's movement.

759 Greif, Jana. LADIES NATIONAL FIDDLE CHAMPION, by Rounder Records, n.d. phonorecord. Rounder Records.

760 HIGH RISK, by Sister Love Productions, n.d. phonorecord. Olivia Records.
The group composed of four women (Bobbi Jackson, Virginia Rubino, Cyndy Mason and Sandi Ajida). The record includes the song "The Common Woman" with words by Judy Grahn and "Degradation" by Donna Deitch.

761 Hood, Janet, and Langford, Linda. JADE AND SARSAPARILLA, by Submaureen Records, n.d. phonorecord. Ladyslipper Music.
An album of very pop sounding gay-identified songs. Most of the songs are about women.

762 IRISH FOLKSONGS FOR WOMEN, by Folkways Records, n.d. phonorecord. Rounder Records.
Traditional Irish folk songs.

763 Jackson, (Aunt) Molly. LIBRARY OF CONGRESS RECORDINGS (1939), by Rounder Records, n.d. phonorecord. Ladyslipper Music.
Aunt Molly Jackson was one of the most influential protest song-writers in the U.S. She helped organize the Appalachian miners in the 1930's. Includes unaccompanied union songs, coal-mining songs, and stories about witches in Kentucky.

764 JAZZ WOMEN: A FEMINIST RETROSPECTIVE, by Stash Records, n.d. Ladyslipper Music.
This anthology of reissues documents the contributions to jazz by women from the 1920's to the early 1940's. There are 34 performances in the two-record set.

Women's Nonprint Media   110

765 Jeritree. HOUSE OF MANY COLORS, by Sea Wave Records, n.d. phonorecord. Ladyslipper Music.
Songs and music by Jeritree (Jeriann Hilderly). Sung and played by her on the marimba with guitar, cello, drums, cymbals, and piano joining in.

766 JO ANN KELLY, by Blue Goose Records, n.d. Rounder Records.
Guitar music.

767 Kaplowitz, Betty. OUT AND ABOUT, by Boof Bray Records, n.d. phonorecord. Ladyslipper Music.
A combination of original and other blues and jazz style songs.

768 Kosse, Roberta. THE RETURN OF THE GREAT MOTHER by ARS Pro Femina, 1978. phonorecord. Ladyslipper Music.
Oratorio composed by Roberta Kosse with text by Jenny Malmquist. It is an impressionistic interpretation of stories from women's herstory through mythology of the Celtic, Egyptian, Greek and early Christian eras. The first movement chronicles women's reality today.

769 LAVENDER JANE LOVES WOMEN, by Women's Wax Works, 1974. phonorecord. Ladyslipper Music.
The first blatantly lesbian album and one of the first to be completely produced and engineered by and for women. A blend of serious and humorous material.

770 Lems, Kristin. BALLAD OF THE ERA, by Carolsdatter Records, n.d. phonorecord (45 rpm). Ladyslipper Music.
A singalong that has become the anthem of many demonstrations and rallies. The other song, "Farmer," is a refutation of ERA foes who say the necessary laws are already on the books.

771 Lems, Kristin. MAMMARY GLANDS, by Carolsdatter Records, n.d. phonorecord (45 rpm). Ladyslipper Music.
A Dixieland jazz band spoof of the exploitive multimillion dollar breast fetish. The other song "Women Walk More Determined" is a more serious tune about women's strength.

772 Lems, Kristin. OH MAMA!, by Carolsdatter Productions, n.d. phonorecord. Carolsdatter Productions.
An album of orignal songs by Kristin Lems.

773 LESBIAN CONCENTRATE, by Olivia Records, n.d. phonorecord. Olivia Records.

An anthology of lesbian music and poetry featuring performances by Linda Tillery, Meg Christian, Cris Williamson, Judy Grahn, Pat Parker, Berkeley Women's Music Collective, Sue Fink, Gwen Avery, BeBe K'Roche, and Mary Watkins.

774 Lilith. BOSTON RIDE, by Galaxia Women Enterprises, 1978. phonorecord. Galaxia Women Enterprises.
A recording of the music of Lilith, an all-woman rock band. The band consists of trumpet, keyboard, fender bass, percussion, saxophone, and guitar. The tunes on this album are "Funky Tale," "Back in Love Again," "Pick up the Pieces," "Boston Ride," "Gold and Silver," "Long Train Runnin'," and "Too Late."

775 McComb, Carol. LOVE CAN TAKE YOU HOME AGAIN, by Bay Records, n.d. phonorecord. Ladyslipper Music.
McComb, a Californian, has roots in traditional music; here she performs her own works accompanied by numerous friends.

776 McNeil, Rita. BORN A WOMAN, by Boot Records, n.d. phonorecord. Ladyslipper Music.
Many of the songs on the album express a powerful political conscience; they echo reels, Scotch ballads and all-night country-western radio stations.

777 Marian McPartland and the All-Women Jazz Ensemble. NOW IS THE TIME, by Halcyon Records, n.d. phonorecord. Ladyslipper Music.
Recordings of the ensemble consisting of McPartland (piano), Vi Redd (sax), Mary Osborne (guitar), Lynn Milano (bass), and Dottie Dodgion (drums).

778 Miyamoto, Joanne Nobuko. A GRAIN OF SAND, by Paredon Records, n.d. phonorecord. Paredon Records.
Nobuko's experiences as a dancer in many top Broadway musicals led her to realize that women of Japanese parentage face a system of racial and sexual stereotyping which must be fought. Turning to singing and composing, she has joined the struggle by Asians in America.

779 Near, Holly. HANG IN THERE, 1973. phonorecord. Redwood Records.
The album, inspired by the anti-war movement, pays musical tribute to the courage of the Vietnamese people. Contains some of Holly's earliest feminist music.

780 Near, Holly. HOLLY NEAR--A LIVE ALBUM, by Redwood Records, n.d. phonorecord. Redwood Records.

Recorded live at the Pitschel Players Cabaret, Los Angeles. Songs include "Started Out Fine," "Old Time Woman," "Laid Off," "Water Came Down," "It Could Have Been Me," "Faces" and "Get Off Me, Baby."
Review: <u>Country Women</u>, December 1976, p57 ("Reflects more of a feminist consciousness than her first album").

781 Near, Holly. IMAGINE MY SURPRISE, by Redwood Records, 1979. phonorecord. Ladyslipper Music.
A very woman-identified album. Contains some country-style music, inspiring political stories, beautiful musical and vocal arrangements by Meg Christian.

782 Near, Holly. YOU CAN KNOW ALL I AM, by Redwood Records, n.d. phonorecord. Redwood Records.
Songs about people's lives. Some of the songs included are "It's My Move," "Song to a Melody," "Someday One Will Do," and "Damn the Poets."
Review: <u>Country Women</u>, December 1976, p57 ("the most 'produced' of Holly's albums").

783 New Harmony Sisterhood Band. ...AND AIN'T I A WOMAN?, by Paredon Records, n.d. phonorecord. Ladyslipper Music.
A 5-woman feminist band whose focus is on political and cultural change.

784 New Haven Women's Liberation Rock Band and Chicago Women's Liberation Rock Band. MOUNTAIN MOVING DAY, by Rounder Records, 1972. phonorecord. Ladyslipper Music.
This record of rock music was one of the first feminist albums.

785 NEW MISS ALICE STONE LADIES SOCIETY ORCHESTRA, by Harmony Club Records, n.d. phonorecord. Harmony Club Records.
A fun, feminist record of Scott Joplin music; also includes original compositions in the ragtime style.

786 THE NEW MISS ALICE STONE LADIES SOCIETY ORCHESTRA, by Harmony Club Records, c.1979. phonorecord. Alice Stone.
A newly released single. The 7 piece, all woman group specializes in satire presented in an eclectic variety of musical forms. Instruments played by the group are: tuba, trombone, clarinet, violin, piano, electric guitar and drums.

787 NEW YORK BASSOON QUARTET, 1979. phonorecord. Leonarda Productions, Inc.

Three of the works were written expressly for this group. The performers, all women, are Bernadette Zirkuli, Jane Taylor, Lauren Goldstein, and Julie Feves. The works are "Colloquy and Chorale" by Alvin Brehm, "Contrasts for Four Bassoons" by Vaclav Nelhybel, "Sinfonia" by Katherine Hoover, and "Last Tango in Beyreuth" by Peter Schickele.

788 Nugent, Trish. FOXGLOVE WOMAN, by Olivia Records, n.d. phonorecord. Olivia Records.
The work of Trish Nugent (songwriter), vocals; Carol Vendrillo, supporting vocals; Marcia Bauman (arranger), piano, harpsichord; Woody Simmons (producer), guitar, banjo. Twelve original songs.

789 Paz, Suni. BROTANDO DEL SILENCIO (BREAKING OUT OF SILENCE), by Paredon Records, 1973. phonorecord. Paredon Records.
Songs of the Latin American struggle for liberation sung in Spanish. Songs about Puerto Rico, Che Guevara, the Chicano movement. Songs of the Latin Women's Liberation Movement and the women of La Raza.

790 Pierce, Ami. WOMANSPIRIT/MORNING STAR, by Pinewood Records, n.d. phonorecord (45 rpm). Ladyslipper Music.
This is the first record by a North Carolina lesbian songwriter/guitarist/performer. It is recorded on her own Pinewood label.

791 Pierson, Suzanne. CHILD, by Souperb Productions, n.d. cassette (60 min). Souperb Productions.
Fifteen songs, including 12 original compositions by Suzanne Pierson recorded in the Republic of South Africa. Some of the songs are "No Child of Mine," "Colorado Homegrown," "I Sow Hay" and "African Omen."

792 PREMIERE: RECORDED PERFORMANCES OF KEYBOARD WORKS BY WOMEN, by Avant Records, n.d. phonorecord. Avant Records.
Compositions written for keyboard instruments by famous women musicians throughout history.
Review: Country Women, December 1976, p56 ("Becoming acquainted with women's best compositions can give us a fresher awareness of the music we've listened to for so long").

793 Reagon, Bernice. GIVE YOUR HANDS TO STRUGGLE: THE EVOLUTION OF A FREEDOM SINGER, by Paredon Records, n.d. phonorecord. Paredon Records.

Bernice Reagon, a founder of the Freedom Singers of SNCC (Student Nonviolent Coordinating Committee), sings all four voices of the female vocal quartet and has composed nearly all the songs.

794 The Red Star Singers. THE FORCE OF LIFE, by Paredon Records, n.d. phonorecord. Paredon Records.
The album features the singing of Bonnie Lockhart where she puts forward comments on contemporary women's problems.

795 Reed, Ola Belle. MY EPITAPH, by Folkways Records, n.d. phonorecord. Rounder Records.
Bluegrass music.

796 Reyes, Judith. MEXICO--DAYS OF STRUGGLE, by Paredon Records, n.d. phonorecord. Paredon Records.
Songs of the unfinished revolution written and sung by Judith Reyes in Spanish. Songs of the Mexican student movement.

797 Reynolds, Malvina. THE JUDGE SAID, by Cassandra Records, n.d. phonorecord (45 rpm). Ladyslipper Music.
This is the song that helped gain support for the petition to recall Wisconsin Judge Archie Simonson after he made inexcusable remarks about how women's dress causes rape and subsequently refused to sentence the rapists of a 16-year-old woman.

798 Reynolds, Malvina. MALVINA, by Cassandra Records. n.d. phonorecord. Schroder Music Company.
Malvina Reynolds sings her own songs, some old favorites and some new songs. Songs include "There's a Bottom Below," "Little Boxes," "You'll Be a Man," and "Turn Around."

799 Reynolds, Malvina. MALVINA--HELD OVER, by Cassandra Records, n.d. phonorecord. Schroder Music Company.
Malvina Reynolds singing "Rosie Jane," "If You Love Me," "What Have They Done to the Rain," "Magic Penny," "The Whale" and more.

800 Reynolds, Malvina. MALVINA REYNOLDS, by Century City Records, n.d. phonorecord. Schroder Music Company.
The Century City album has, among other songs, "We Hate to See Them Go," "World Gone Beautiful," "It Isn't Nice" and "Morningtown Ride."

Recordings/Music

801 Romaine, Anne. GETTIN' ON COUNTRY, by Rounder Records, n.d. phonorecord. Rounder Records.
Country and feminist music.

802 SARAH OGUN GUNNING, by Rounder Records, n.d. phonorecord, Rounder Records.
Includes some mining and anti-capitalist songs.

803 Seeger, Peggy. PENELOPE ISN'T WAITING ANY MORE, by Rounder Records, n.d. phonorecord. Ladyslipper Music.
An album of mostly traditional American women's songs arranged and sung by Peggy.

804 Shear, Linda. A LESBIAN PORTRAIT, by Old Lady Blue Jeans, n.d. cassette or reel-to-reel. Old Lady Blue Jeans.
Linda Shear seeks out our spiritual and earthly presence through startling musical images. A combination of voice and piano.

805 Simmons, Woody. OREGON MOUNTAINS, by Olivia Records, n.d. phonorecord. Olivia Records.
Predominantly country and bluegrass--influenced by old-time jazz and swing. Ten original songs.

806 Simons, Nelly. PIED PIPER OF HAMELIN/PUDDIN-TAMEL/SET OF POEMS FOR CHILDREN, by Ladyslipper Music, n.d. phonorecord. Ladyslipper Music.

807 Spiegel, Laurie. LAURIE SPIEGEL, VOLUME ONE, 1979. phonorecord. Leonarda Productions, Inc.
The album consists of some of her works written from 1974 to 1976, all of it electronic music. The works are "Drums," "Pentachrome," "Patchwork" and "The Expanding Universe."

808 Stewart, Lucy. SCOTTISH BALLADS, by Folkways Records, n.d. phonorecord. Rounder Records.

809 SURVEY OF AMERICAN WOMEN COMPOSERS, by CRI Records, n.d. phonorecord. Ladyslipper Music.
Classical compositions by five American women composers: Mabel Daniels, Louise Talma, Vivian Fine, Julia Perry and Mary Howe.

810 SWEET HONEY IN THE ROCK, by Flying Fish Records, n.d. phonorecord. Ladyslipper Music.
Five black women singing a cappella. The songs range from gospel to love songs to those with a specific political message.

811 Sweet Honey in the Rock. B'LIEVE I'll RUN ON...SEE WHAT THE END'S GONNA BE, by Redwood Records, 1978. phonorecord. Ladyslipper Music.
Second album from this group. The songs, many of them written by the group, talk about the experiences of black women, social injustice, and specific strong black women.

812 Tabor, Jane. AIR AND GRACES, by Tropic Records, n.d. phonorecord. Rounder Records.
Traditional English folksongs.

813 Tillery, Linda. LINDA TILLERY, by Olivia Records, n.d. phonorecord. Olivia Records.

814 Trull, Teresa. THE WAYS A WOMAN CAN BE, by Olivia Records, n.d. phonorecord. Olivia Records.
Teresa Trull is a singer/songwriter and guitarist whose music utilizes the pop/blues/country influences of her Southern roots.

815 Tyson, Willie. DEBUTANTE, by Urana Records, n.d. phonorecord. Ladyslipper Music.
Blues and ballads, mostly written by Tyson. The songs are humorous, sarcastic and clever.

816 Tyson, Willie. FULL COUNT, by Lima Bean Records, n.d. phonorecord. Lima Bean Records.
An album of feminist rock. One song, "The Ballad of Merciful Mary," is an account of the injustice shown rape victims.
Reviews: <u>Country Women</u>, December 1976, p57 ("Willie has a deep, captivating voice that pulls you into her songs"). <u>Paid My Dues</u>, October 1975, p24.

817 VIRGO RISING: THE ONCE AND FUTURE WOMAN, by Thunderbird Records, n.d. phonorecord. Thunderbird Records.
Seven women produce an album that reveals women's diversity and reflects their own worth. They sing about the growing awareness of what is--and of what can be.

818 Voss, Jane. AN ALBUM OF SONGS, by Bay Records, n.d. phonorecord. Bay Records.
Jane sings and plays old-time country music. Some of the songs included are "Goodbye to My Stepstone," "Clinch Mountain Home" and "Bear Creek Blues."

819 Warren, Elinor Remick. ABRAM IN EGYPT/SUITE FOR ORCHESTRA, by Ladyslipper Music, n.d. phonorecord. Ladyslipper Music.

820 Watkins, Mary. MARY WATKINS: SOMETHING MOVING, by Olivia Records, n.d. phonorecord. Olivia Records.
The piano and songs of Mary Watkins.

821 WHAT NOW, PEOPLE #1, by Paredon Records, n.d. phonorecord. Paredon Records.
The album is a collection of the work of several women. Included are Holly Near, Beverly Grant, Muriel Hogan, Nancy Rhodes, Bernice Reagon and Barbara Dane.

822 WHEN WOMEN SANG THE BLUES, by Blues Classics, n.d. phonorecord. Ladyslipper Music.
Anthology of blues reissues, all sung by women.

823 Williamson, Chris. THE CHANGER AND THE CHANGED, n.d. phonorecord or cassette. Olivia Records.
Chris Williamson plays piano and guitar and performs her own music as well as the music of her contemporaries. The album varies in sound from solo piano and voice to a joyous chorus, from a country band to rich strings.
Review: Country Women, December 1976, p57 ("Chris is concerned with spirituality and her music reflects that, as well as her roots--the wide open country").

824 Williamson, Chris. LIVE DREAM, by Olivia Records, n.d. phonorecord. Olivia Records.
Composed of live performances taken from two years of various women-produced concerts across the United States.

825 WOMAN'S WORK: WORKS BY FAMOUS WOMEN COMPOSERS, by Marnie Hall, 1975. phonorecord. Gemini Hall Records.
Contains three centuries of work by 18 European women composers. The music ranges from piano music to various combinations involving voice, strings, piano, and harpsichord. A 44-page booklet contains biographical material on the composers.
Review: Feminist Art Journal, spring 1976, p43-4 ("There is much, much more music by women of the past as well as of the present, which deserves to be recorded. Woman's Work is a welcome beginning"--Barbara Jepson).

826 WOMEN IN JAZZ: ALL WOMEN BANDS, by Stash Records, n.d. phonorecord. Ladyslipper Music.
Jazz reissues. Mary Lou Williams, Mary Osborne, Margie Hyams, Vivian Garry, Beryl Booker, Terry Pollard, Norma Carson, L'Ana Hyams, International Sweethearts of Jazz--recorded 1945-1954. (This is volume 1 of a set; entry 827 is volume 2 and entry 828 is volume 3.)

827 WOMEN IN JAZZ: PIANISTS, by Stash Records, n.d. phonorecord. Ladyslipper Music.
   Jazz reissues. Volume 2 (826 is volume 1; 828 is volume 3) includes Mary Lou Williams, Arizona Dranes, Lovie Austin, Lil Hardin Armstrong, Una Mae Carlisle, Jutta Hyip.

828 WOMEN IN JAZZ: SWINGTIME TO MODERN, by Stash Records, n.d. phonorecord. Ladyslipper Music.
   Jazz reissues. Volume 3 (volume 1 is entry 826 and volume 2, 827) includes L'Ana Hyams, Margie Hyams, Valaida Snow, Una Mae Carlisle, Kathy Stobart, Jutta Hyip, Beryl Booker, Terry Pollard, Vi Redd, International Sweethearts of Rhythm.

829 Zaimont, Judith Lang. MUSIC BY JUDITH LANG ZAIMONT, 1979. phonorecord. Leonarda Productions, Inc.
   Ms. Laimont defines herself as a neo-Romantic composer. The album consists of "A Calendar Set," 12 preludes for solo piano, "Chansons Nobles et Sentimentales," and "Nocturne La Fin de Siècle."

CONTEMPORARY FILMMAKERS' WORKS

830 Aaron, Jane. IN PLAIN SIGHT, 1977. 3 min. color. Serious Business Company.
The real world jitters in pixillated motion juxtaposed with the movement of drawn animation.

831 Anderson, Madeline. BEING ME, 1975. 20 min. color. Phoenix Films.
Documentary about children.

832 Beams, Mary. DROWNING MOON, 1975. 45 seconds. b/w. Serious Business Company.
Line animation; comedy.

833 Beams, Mary. GOING HOME SKETCHBOOK, 1975. 3 min. color. Serious Business Company.
Animated; abstract cine-poem, rotoscope technique.

834 Beams, Mary. PAUL REVERE IS HERE, 1976. 7 min. color. Serious Business Compay.
Animated, rotoscope technique.

835 Beams, Mary. PIANO RUB, 1975. 3 min. color. Serious Business Company.
Animated; abstract shapes and subjects.

836 Beams, Mary SEED REEL, 1975. 4 min. b/w. Serious Business Company.
Animated comedy.

837 Beams, Mary. SOLO, 1975. 2 min. b/w. Serious Business Company.
Line animation; abstract.

838 Borenstein, Joyce. REVISITED, 1976. 8 min. color. Creative Film Society.
A combination of animation and live action filming. Revisited is a journey into the unconscious mind.

839 Cox, Nell. KENTUCKY MURDER TRIAL, 1976. 58 min. color. Soho.

Documentary of a murder trial.

840 Crafts, Lisa. DESIRE PIE, 1977. 4½ min. color. Serious Business Company.
An animated celebration of lovemaking.

841 Cruikshank, Sally. QUASI AT THE QUACKADERO, 1975. 10 min. color. Serious Business Company.
Quasi, his girlfriend Anita, and mechanical dog Rollo visit the Quackadero, a futuristic amusement park. Animated.

842 Cruikshank, Sally. MAKE ME PSYCHIC, 1979. 8 min. color. Serious Business Company.
The trio of Quasi, Anita and Rollo return in this stylized art deco-looking sequel to Quasi.

843 Dail, Marija Miletic. WHY NOT?, 1973. 6 min. color. Creative Film Society.
An animated film featuring a family, and the parents in particular, who lapse into wondrous realms of fantasy while performing routine tasks.

844 Doray, Audrey. ZODIAC, 1972. 9 min. color. Douglas College.
Animated.

845 Gomez, Andrea. NIGUN, 1977. 9 min. color. Serious Business Company.
The story of a primordial couple and the birth of their child, set to a chantlike sound track by Harry Partch.

846 Haleff, Maxine. THE MAGIC LANTERN MOVIE, n.d. 9 min. color. Serious Business Company.
A history of the magic lantern, forerunner of the motion picture projector, and its entertainment uses in vaudeville, theatre, and the home.

847 Hallett, Judith Divan. I LOVE TO BE HAPPY, 1976. 30 min. color. Soho.
Documentary of community dance groups.

848 Hays, Lora, and Stoia, Renata. BOY AND A BOA, 1975. 13 min. color. Phoenix Films.
Animated story.

849 Hochberg, Victoria. ANGEL THIGHS: LES BALLET TROCKADERO DE MONTE CARLO, 1975. 15 min. color. Victoria Hochberg.
Documentary of an all male ballerina company.

850 Hochberg, Victoria. METROLINER, 1976. 35 min. color. Victoria Hochberg.
A documentary of the American railroad.
Review: Booklist, January 15, 1977, p728-9 ("the filmmaker and her crew should be applauded for their noteworthy execution of the concept. Far too many films lack this balance, fresh approach and technical execution" --Beth Ann Herbert).

851 Hornisher, Christina. 4 BY 8=16, n.d. 3 min. color. Creative Films.
Optical printing technique.

852 Hubley, Faith. SECOND CHANCE: SEA, 1976. 11 min. color. Pyramid Films.
Animated film portraying the evolution of the oceans, their influence on civilizations and the events leading to their present precarious state.

853 Hubley, Faith. WHITHER WEATHER, 1978. 11 min. color. Pyramid Films.
Using animation techniques, the filmmaker shows how people inter-relate with their world.

854 Johnson, Karen. ORANGE, 1970. 3 min. color. Serious Business Company.
A carefully selected point of view of the eating of an orange. Macro-photography.

855 Klosky, Linda. AND THEN THERE WERE, 1973. 3 min. color. Iris Films.
Animated film using a mosaic technique, showing how nature destroys and refurbishes itself and humankind destroys. Good environmental short.

856 Li, Diane. THE BAREFOOT DOCTORS, 1975. 52 min. color. Diane Li Productions.
A documentary focusing on the training and activities of "barefoot doctors" in People's Republic of China."
Review: Booklist, May 1, 1975, p1274 ("covers the subject well....an interesting production"--Mark Zweigler).

857 Minot, Gabrielle. CATS IN THE DARK, 1973. 3 min. color. Douglas College.
Animated fantasy.

858 Nelson, Gunvor. TROLLSTENEN, 1976. 125 min. color. Serious Business Company.
A stylized portrait of her family as they recall their childhood in Sweden.

859 Orr, Diane. THE LONGEST WAR, 1976. 30 min. color. Soho.
Documentary filmed from inside the compound during the takeover at Wounded Knee.

860 Petty, Sara. FURIES, 1977. 3 min. color. Creative Film Society.
Executed in charcoal and pastel on paper, this animated short is a graphic expression of the intense experience of the cat. The film is largely non-representational, an expression of the furtive, nervous state of cats.

861 Petty, Sara. SHADRAC, 1977. 2 min. color. Creative Film Society.
A continual metamorphosis of abstract shapes, faces, and animal forms. The images have been drawn with charcoal and pastel.

862 Ramstad, Josie. BIRD LADY vs. THE GALLOPING GONADS, 1976. 2 min. b/w. Serious Business Company.
Line animation; fantasy.

863 Rose, Kathy. ARTS CIRCUS, n.d. 4 min. color. Creative Films.
Animated fantasy.

864 Rose, Kathy. THE DOODLERS, 1976. 5 min. color. Serious Business Company.
Animated comedy.

865 Rose, Kathy. MIRROR PEOPLE, 1974. 4 min. color. Serious Business Company.
Animated fantasy.

866 Rose, Kathy. MOON SHOW, n.d. 2 min. color. Creative Films.
Abstract forms.

867 Rose, Kathy. THE MYSTERIANS, 1973. 6 min. color. Serious Business Company.
Animated fantasy.

868 Rose, Kathy. PENCIL BOOKLINGS, 1978. 14 min. color. Serious Business Company.
Animated film about the relationships of an artist to her material.

869 Ross, Marsha. RAINDANCE, 1977. 8 min. color. Creative Film Society.
A visual poem of imagery, done with double exposure.

870 Severson, Annie. STRUGGLE OF THE MEAT, 1974. 3 min. color. Serious Business Company.
Primarily abstract images with some wildlife footage.

871 Smith, Sandy. SUPERNUMERARIES, 1976. 16 min. b/w. Iris Films.
The occasion of a performance allows a group of women and one man to suspend their traditional self images and deal with their costumed anonymity.

872 Spears, Helyn. THE CREATURES IN MY GARAGE, 1976. 3 min. color. Creative Film Society.
Animated tale about a little boy and the magical animals that inhabit his garage.

873 Strand, Chick. COSAS DE MI VIDA, 1976. 23 min. color. Serious Business Company.
Documentary portrait of Anselmo, a Mexican man, born into poverty and orphaned at age seven.

874 Strand, Chick. ELASTICITY, 1976. 22 min. color. Serious Business Company.
Experimental editing; sounds and images from American scenes.

875 Strand, Chick. GUACAMOLE, 1976. 10 min. color. Serious Business Company.
Focuses on the Mexican fiesta and bullfight; a cine-poem.

876 Wolff, Peggy. 108 MOVEMENTS, n.d. 6 min. color. Creative Films.
Experimental editing.

DIRECTORY OF DISTRIBUTORS

Indra Allen
Cell 16
22 Ashcroft Road
Medford MA 02155

Max Almy and Barbara
  Hammer
1556 Noe St
San Francisco CA 94131

American Alliance for Health,
  Physical Education, and
    Recreation
c/o NEA Sound Studios
1201 16th St NW
Washington DC 20036

American Library Color
  Slide Co.
222 W 23d St
New York NY 10011

Argo Records
539 W 25th St
New York NY 10001

Marta Segovia Ashley
  (Femedia)
240 Alma St
San Francisco CA
  Also available from
    Satellite Video Exchange
      Society
    261 Powell St
    Vancouver BC Canada

Asian-American Theatre
  Workshop
Seattle WA
  Also available from
    Satellite Video Exchange
      Society
    261 Powell St
    Vancouver BC Canada

Athletic Institute
705 Merchandise Mart
Chicago IL 60654

Audio Lingual Educational
  Press
217 Laurel Rd
Northport NY 11768

Avant Records
6331 Quebec Dr
Hollywood CA 90068

BFA Educational Media
2211 Michigan Ave
Santa Monica CA 90406

BFC-TV Film Library
Room 864
475 Riverside Dr
New York NY 10027

Bay Records
1516 Oak St
Suite 320
Alameda CA 94501

Alan Bloom
115 6th St #6
San Rafael CA 94901

Blue Ridge Films
9003 Glenbrook Rd
Fairfax VA 22030

June Boe
RR #2
Gibson BC Canada
  Also available from
    Satellite Video Exchange
      Society
    261 Powell St
    Vancouver BC Canada

Distributors

Boot Records
1818 Division St
Nashville TN 37203

Barbara Boxer
PO Box 1048
San Rafael CA 94901

Brigham Young University
Provo UT 84602

Bro-Dart
1609 Memorial Ave
Williamsport PA 17701

Miller Brody
342 Madison Ave
New York NY 10017

Audrey Bryant
Video Women and Film
223 12th Ave SW
Calgary AB Canada
  Also available from
  Satellite Video Exchange
    Society
  261 Powell St
  Vancouver BC Canada

Butterick Publishing
181 Ave of Americas
New York NY 10013

Caedmon Records
505 8th Ave
New York NY 10018

Cambridge Documentary
  Films
PO Box 385
Cambridge MA 02139

Peg Campbell
1421 7th Ave
New Westminster BC Canada
  Also available from
  Satellite Video Exchange
    Society
  261 Powell St
  Vancouver BC Canada

Canadian Women TV Series
Gail Valaskakis
c/o YWCA
1355 Dorchester Blvd W
Montreal QB Canada
  Also available from
  Satellite Video Exchange
    Society
  261 Powell St
  Vancouver BC Canada

Carolsdatter Publications
908 W California #3
Urbana IL 61801

Carousel Films
1501 Broadway
New York NY 10036

Center for Humanities
2 Holland Ave
White Plains NY 10603

Churchill Films
662 N Robertson Blvd
Los Angeles CA 90069

Consumnes River College
8401 Center Parkway
Sacramento CA 95823

Martha Coolidge
236 19th St
New York NY 10003

Coronet Instructional
  Media
65 E South Water St
Chicago IL 60601

Creative Film Society
7237 Canby Ave
Reseda CA 91335

Leigh Deering/Mary Gillies
1026 Clark Dr
Vancouver BC Canada
  Also available from
  Satellite Video Exchange
    Society
  261 Powell St
  Vancouver BC Canada

Doubleday Multimedia
Garden City NY 11530

Douglas College
PO Box 2503
New Westminster BC
  Canada

Educational Activities
Box 392
Freeport NY 11520

Educational Audio Visual
Pleasantville NY 10570

Educational Dimensions Group
Box 126
Stamford CT 06904

Educational Records
157 Chambers St
New York NY 10007

Eggplant Media Productions
PO Box 14001
Hartford CT 06114

Encyclopaedia Britannica
425 N Michigan Ave
Chicago IL 60611

Everett/Edwards
PO Box 1060
Deland FL 32720

Eye Gate Media
146-01 Archer Ave
Jamaica NY 11435

Feminist History Research
  Project
Box 1156
Topanga CA 90290

Feminist Productions
23 Whalers Cove
Babylon NY 11702

Feminist Radio Network
PO Box 5537
Washington DC 20016

Femme Films, Inc.
4537 Grand Ave S
Minneapolis MN 55409

Film Classic Exchange
1926 S Vermont Ave
Los Angeles CA 90007

Films for the Humanities
Box 2053
Princeton NJ 08540

Films Incorporated
1144 Wilmette Ave
Wilmette IL 60091

Folkways Records
701 Seventh Avenue
New York NY 10036

Suzanne C. Fox
1815 Stuart St
Berkeley CA 94703

Galaxia Women Enterprises
Box 212
Woburn MA 01801

Dr. Alan Garfield
Director
St. Joseph Art Center
St. Joseph MI 49085

Michelle Gebhardt Film Co.
1380 Bush St
San Francisco CA 94109

Gemini Hall Records
808 West End Ave
New York NY 10025

Global Village
454 Broome St
New York NY 10012

Leni Goldberg
8535 Appian Way
Hollywood CA 90046
  Also available from
  Satellite Video Exchange
    Society
  261 Powell St
  Vancouver BC Canada

Distributors

Grove Press
196 W Houston St
New York NY 10014

Guidance Associates
757 Third Ave
New York NY 10017

Irene Halikas
3567 Girouard
Montreal QB Canada
  Also available from
  Satellite Video Exchange
    Society
  261 Powell St
  Vancouver BC Canada

Harmony Club Records
Box 925
Hollywood CA 90028

Harper & Row
10 E 53d St
New York NY 10022

Caroline F. Hatch
448 Taraval #2
San Francisco CA 94116

Victoria Hochberg
  Productions
6825 Alta Loma Terr
Hollywood CA 90068

Indiana University
Audiovisual Center
Bloomington IN 47401

Innerflex Media
816 Spring St
Ann Arbor MI 48103

Insight Exchange
Box 42584
San Francisco CA 94101

Iris Films
Iris Feminist Collective, Inc.
Box 5353
Berkeley CA 94705

Valle Jones/Spectra Feminist
  Media

115 8th St SE
Washington DC 20003

KUT-FM
Box 7158
University of Texas
Austin TX 78712

Kartemquin/Haymarket Films
PO Box 1665
Evanston IL 60204

L.A. Women's Video Center
The Woman's Building
1727 N Spring St
Los Angeles CA 90012

Ladyslipper Music
PO Box 3124
Durham NC 27705

Lansford Publishing Co.
Box 8711
San Jose CA 95155

Learning Corporation of
  America
1350 Ave of Americas
New York NY 10019

Leonarda Productions, Inc.
PO Box 124
Radio City Station
New York NY 10019

Diane Li Productions
PO Box 2110
Stanford CA 94305

Lima Bean Records
217 12th St SE
Washington DC 20003

Los Angeles Feminist Video
  Outlet
PO Box 5114
Santa Monica CA 90405

Lucern Films
200 Winston Dr
Suite 1415
Cliffside Park NJ 07010

Distributors

Mainstream International
Philadelphia PA

Mass Communications, Inc.
25 Sylvan Rd
Westport CT   06880

Masters and Masterworks
   Productions
Box 1410
Pacific Palisades CA   90272

Mauritamusic
34 Norwood Dr
Normal IL   61761

McGraw-Hill Films
1221 Ave of Americas
New York NY   10020

Robert Mickelson
1107 W 54th Ave
Vancouver BC   Canada
   Also available from
   Satellite Video Exchange
      Society
   261 Powell St
   Vancouver BC   Canada

Arthur Mokin Productions
17 W 60th St
New York NY   10023

Moonforce Media
PO Box 2934
Main City Sta
Washington DC   20013

Moreland-Latchford
   Productions
299 Queen St W
Toronto ON   Canada

Multi-Media Productions
Box 5097
Stanford CA   94305

National Audiovisual Center
Washington DC   20409

National Council of Churches
TV Film Library
Room 860
475 Riverside Dr
New York NY   10027

National Film Board of Canada
1251 Ave of Americas
New York NY   10020

National Insitute of Education
   Development Center
55 Chapel St
Newton MA   02160

New Day Films
Box 315
Franklin Lakes NJ   07417

New Line Cinema
853 Broadway
New York NY   10003

Maireen Newell
45 Jason St
Arlington MA   02174

Newsreel Films
26 W 20th St
New York NY   10011

Jeffrey Norton Publishers
145 E 49th St
New York NY   10017

Odeon Films
PO Box 315
Franklin Lakes NJ   07417

Old Lady Blue Jeans
200 Main St
Northampton MA   01060

Olesen
1535 Ivar Ave
Hollywood CA   90028

Olivia Records
Box 70237
Los Angeles CA   90070

Optic Nerve
141 10th St
San Francisco CA   94703

Distributors

Pacifica Tape Library
5316 Venice Blvd
Los Angeles CA 90019

Paredon Records
Box 889
Brooklyn NY 11202

Pathescope Educational
  Media
71 Weyman Ave
New Rochelle NY 10802

Perfection Form Co.
214 W 8th St
Logan CA

Perspective Films
214 W Erie St
Chicago IL 60610

Phantom Records
1790 Broadway
New York NY 10019

Phoenix Films
470 Park Ave S
New York NY 10016

Pleiades Records
PO Box 7217
Berkeley CA 94707

Polydor Records
1700 Broadway
New York NY 10019

Portable Channel
8 Prince St
Rochester NY 14607

Public Television Library
475 L'Enfant Plaza SW
Washington DC 20024

Pyramid Films
Box 1048
Santa Monica CA 90406

Red Hen Films
1305 Oxford St
Berkeley CA 94709

Redwood Records
565 Doolin Canyon Rd
Ukiah CA 95482

Reel Feelings
4973 Angus Dr
Vancouver BC Canada
  Also available from
  Satellite Video Exchange
    Society
  261 Powell St
  Vancouver BC Canada

Jon Rosen
60 Knolls Crescent
Bronx NY 10463

Rosenthal Art Slides
5456 S Ridgewood Court
Chicago IL 60615

Rounder Records
186 Willow Ave
Somerville MA 02144

Rebecca Rubens
Box 310 Rt 3
Astoria OR 97103

Satellite Video Exchange
  Society
261 Powell St
Vancouver BC Canada

Schloat Productions
150 White Plains Rd
Tarrytown NY 10591

Schroder Music Co.
2027 Parker
Berkeley CA 94704

Robin Schwartz
67 Second Ave
New York NY 10003

Serious Business Co.
1145 Madana Blvd
Oakland CA 94610

Shameless Hussy Press
Box 424
San Lorenzo CA 94580

Mo Simpson
2215 W 5th Ave
Vancouver BC Canada
  Also available from
  Satellite Video Exchange
    Society
  261 Powell St
  Vancouver BC Canada

Sisters Unlimited
1492F Willow Lake Dr
Atlanta GA 30329

Society for Nutrition
  Education
Suite 1110
2140 Shattuck Ave
Berkeley CA 94704

Soho Cinema
225 Lafayette St
New York NY 10012

Souperb Productions
46 Skyline Dr
Denver CO 80215

Alice Stone
PO Box 925
Hollywood CA 90028

Martha Stuart
  Communications
66 Bank St
New York NY 10014

Gail Swanson
65 San Carlos
Sausalito CA 94965

Sweet Alliance
Box 2879
Washington DC 20013

Teaching Resources Films
2 Kisco Plaza
Mt. Kisco NY 10549

TeleKETICS
1229 S Santee
Los Angeles CA 90015

Terpsichore Distributing
3495 Bodega Ave
Petaluma CA 94952

Texture Films
1600 Broadway
New York NY 10019

Third Eye Films
12 Arrow St
Cambridge MA 02138

Thunderbird Records
326 Flint St
Reno NV 89501

Time-Life Multi Media
Time and Life Building
Rockefeller Center
New York NY 10020

Tomatoe Productions
Box 1952
Evergreen CO 80439

Transition House Films
120 Boylston St
Boston MA 02116

Tricontinental Film Center
333 Sixth Ave
New York NY 10014

United Nations
Radio and Visual Services
New York NY 10017

University of California
Extension Media Center
2223 Fulton St
Berkeley CA 94720

University of South Florida
Division of Educational
  Resources
Film Library
Tampa FL 33620

University of South Florida
Women's Studies Program
Tampa FL 33620

Distributors

University of Southern California
Department of Cinema
University Park CA 90007

Linda Vance
Women's Centre, YWCA
1355 Dorchester Blvd W
Montreal QB Canada
  Also available from
  Satellite Video Exchange
    Society
  261 Powell St
  Vancouver BC Canada

Vediamo Productions
46 Ann St
New York NY 10038

Video Inn
261 Powell St
Vancouver BC Canada

Vulva Video
PO Box 5114
Santa Monica CA 90405

WGBH Educational
  Foundation
125 Western Ave
Boston MA 02134

WTL Productions
111 Raymond Blvd
Newark NJ 07102

H.W. Wilson Corporation
555 W Taft Dr
South Holland IL 60437

Wise Women Enterprises
20 W 22d St   Room 612
New York NY 10010

Wombat Productions
77 Tarrytown Rd
White Plains NY 10607

Women Alive, Cable 10
c/o British Columbia Status
  of Women
Vancouver BC Canada

Also available from
Satellite Video Exchange
  Society
261 Powell St
Vancouver BC Canada

Women and Work Video
Box 122
Chelsea MI 48118

Women in Focus
#6-45 Kingsway
Vancouver BC Canada

Women in Newspaper
  Management
School of Journalism
Indiana University
Bloomington IN 47405

Women Make Movies
257 W 19th St
New York NY 10011

Women Make Movies
779 Susquehanna Ave
Franklin Lakes NJ 07417

Women on Words and Images
Box 2163
Princeton NJ 08504

The Women's Audio Exchange
49 W Main St
Cambridge NY 12816

Women's Center, YWCA
1355 Dorchester Blvd W
Montreal QB Canada
  Also available from
  Satellite Video Exchange
    Society
  261 Powell St
  Vancouver BC Canada

Women's Eye Multi Media
  Productions
7909 Sycamore Dr
Falls Church VA 22402

Women's Film Coop
200 Main St
Northampton MA 01060

Women's Film Project
PO Box 315
Franklin Lakes NJ   07417

Women's Involvement Program
c/o Francie Wyland
100 Bain Ave #57
Toronto ON   Canada
  Also available from
  Satellite Video Exchange
    Society
  261 Powell St
  Vancouver BC   Canada

Women's Involvement Program
c/o Lyn Wright
99 Enderby Road
Toronto, ON   Canada
  Also available from
  Satellite Video Exchange
    Society
  261 Powell St
  Vancouver BC   Canada

YWCA of Canada
571 Jarvis St
Toronto ON   Canada

ADDITIONAL RESOURCES

Association of American Colleges. Women and Film: A Resource Handbook. Washington, D.C.: The Association, 1974.

Barnett, Joan, and Ann Pettingill. Women: A Bibliography of Books and Other Materials. Los Angeles: John F. Kennedy Memorial Library, California State University, 1975.

Betencourt, Jeanne. Women in Focus. Dayton, Ohio: Pflaum, Standard, 1974.

Dawson, Bonnie. Women's Film in Print: An Annotated Guide to Over 750 Films. San Francisco: Booklegger Press, 1975.

Edwards, Richard, and Bruce Gronbeck. A Partial List of Educational, Instructional and Documentary Films Treating Women's Roles, Problems, and Communication Strategies. Washington, D.C.: ERIC, 1975.

Emmens, Carol. Famous People on Film. Metuchen, N.J.: Scarecrow Press, 1977.

Garrard, Mary D. Slides of Works by Women Artists: A Source Book. Washington, D.C.: The Author, 1974. (Available from Mary Garrard, 4907 Upton St NW, Washington DC 20016)

Harrison, Cynthia. Women's Movement Media: A Sourcebook. New York: Bowker, 1975.

Kowalski, Rosemary. Women and Film: A Bibliography. Metuchen, N.J.: Scarecrow Press, 1976.

Media Report to Women Directory. Washington, D.C.: Women's Institute for Freedom of the Press, annual.

My Sister's Song: Women's Records. Milwaukee: Women's Soul Publishing, 1975.

Navaretta, Cynthia, editor. Guide to Women's Art Organizations: Groups/Activities/Networks/Publications. New York: Midmarch Associates, 1979.

Additional Resources 135

We Shall Go Forth: 1979 Directory of Resources in Women's Music. (Available from Toni Armstrong, 6721 N Glenwood, Chicago IL 60626)

Wheeler, Helen. Womanhood Media, 1969; Supplement 1975. Metuchen, N.J.: Scarecrow Press, 1975.

Women's Films--A Critical Guide. Bloomington: Indiana University Press, 1975.

Women's History Research Center. Directory of Films by and about Women. Berkeley, Calif.: The Center, 1972.

SUBJECT INDEX

ABORTION see BIRTH CONTROL...

ACTRESSES see DRAMA...

ADOLESCENCE
    16mm Films 67
    Videotapes 330
    Recordings/Spoken 468

AGEISM (Age Discrimination)
    Videotapes 204, 205, 206
    Recordings/Spoken 585

ALCOHOLISM
    Slides 457

ART, ARTISTS
    16mm Films 35; Chase, Doris 33, 65; Kahlo, Frida 101; Maynard, Valerie 159; Neel, Alice 153; Varo, Remedios 137
    Videotapes 251, 260, 289, 325, 346, 351, 354, 359
    Filmstrips 379
    Slides 425, 433, 445, 458, 459, 460, 461, 462, 463; Bacon, Peggy 421; Bauermeister, Mary 419; Bry, Edith 432; Cassatt, Mary 420, 422; Fine, Perle 423; Fuller, Sue 424; Gerardia, Helen 436; Greenwood, Marion 418; Morisot, Berthe 426, 427, 428; O'Keeffe, Georgia 415, 435; Pereira, I. Rice 416; Zevon, Irene 417
    Recordings/Spoken 523, 611, 658, 681, 691; Brooks, Romaine 613; Chicago, Judy 536; Grey, Eileen 513; Nemser, Cindy 500; Shapiro, Miriam 536

AUTHORS see LITERATURE...

BATTERED WOMEN (see also VIOLENCE)
    16mm Films 15, 16, 166, 171
    Videotapes 207, 210, 211, 222, 257, 311, 320, 341
    Slides 454
    Recordings/Spoken 469

BIOGRAPHY
    16mm Films (General) 113, 138, 155, 200; Anderson,

Annie 45; Argoff, Rose 140; Atkinson, Ti-Grace, 146; Brown, Rita Mae 146; Catherine of Siena 44; Chisholm, Shirley 31; Covington, Lucy 107; Crater, Flora 175; Cunningham, Imogen 87, 88; Davis, Cathy "Cat" 26; Elizabeth I of England 44; Flanner, Janet 196; Fox, Margaret Fell 44; Friedan, Betty 146; Goldsmith, Grace A., M.D. 98; Guggenheim, Peggy 130; Hansberry, Lorraine 105; Jackson, Mahalia 109; Jefferson, Margo 146; Jordan, Crystal Lee 39; Kahlo, Frida 101; Karp, Lila 146; Korbut, Olga, 123; Maynard, Valerie 159; Millet, Kate 146; Morrison, Toni 196; Neel, Alice 153; Nin, Anais 9; Noble, Elaine 180; Nyad, Diana 38; Pinckney, Eliza Lucas 52; Reynolds, Malvina 106; Rukeyser, Muriel 153, 196; Sampson, Deborah 43; Shaw, George Bernard 181; Sokolow, Anna 153; Stout, Ruth 142; Taussig, Helen, M.D. 99; Varo, Remedios 137; Welty, Eudora 196; Wong, Jade Snow 91; Zell, Katherin 44; Zilkha, Louise 119

<u>Videotapes</u> (General) 217, 249, 261, 279, 310, 318, 335; Anguissola, Sofonisba 251; Atkinson, Ti-Grace 331; Atwood, Margaret 280; Beauvoir, Simone de 233; Bishop, Isabel 351; Bond, Victoria 350; Bonheur, Rosa 351; Boulanger, Lili 350; Bramlett, Betty Jane 351; Brown, Eileen 243; Caccini, Francesca 350; Carriera, Rosalba 251, 351; Charpentier, Constance Marie 251; Coulthard, Jean 350; Eckhardt-Grammate, Sonia 350; Ferron 245; Fontana, Lavinia 251; Gambioli, Joan 325; Garcia, Inez 299; Gentileschi, Artemisia 251, 351; Ghisi, Diana 351; Gorton, Ruthie 312; Groesbeck, Arvilla 208; Herschel, Caroline 218; Holmes, Tiffany 362; Jacobi, Lotte 231; Jancic, Olga 325; Jessye, Eva 237; Johnson, Henrietta 351; Kaplowitz, Betty 212; Kauffman, Angelica 251; Kubach-Wilmsen, Anna-Maria 325; Labille-Guiard, Adelaide 251; Leyster, Judith 251, 351; Lord, Audre 229; Mead, Margaret 281; Mendelssohn, Fanny 350; Merian, Maria Sibylla 251; Millet, Kate 264; Moreau, Jeanne 230; Morgan, Robin 232; Nelli, Plautilla 351; Oliphant, Sara 351; Opliger, Pamela 351; Osborne, Nancy 351; Paradis, Maria Theresa von 350; Pentland, Barbara 350; Piercy, Marge 229; Richards, Beah 258; Robusti, Marietta 351; Ruysch, Rachel 251; Schafer, Ann 265; Schumann, Clara Wieck 350; Shange, Ntozake 246; Steinbock, Sabina von 351; Stevens, May 351; Tailleferre, Germaine 350; Van Henessen, Catharina 251; Velasquez, Elaine 352; Vigee-Lebrun, Elizabeth 251, 351; Wanrow, Yvonne 370

<u>Filmstrips</u> (General) 391; Cather, Willa 398, 412; Escobar, Marisol 379; Frankenthaler, Helen 379; Glasgow, Ellen 412; Hatshepsut 380; Nevelson, Louise 379; O'Keeffe, Georgia 379; Wharton, Edith 412

<u>Slides</u>   Paul, Alice 450

Recordings/Spoken (General) 713; Alcott, Louisa May 496; Anthony, Susan B. 518; Austen, Jane 590; Baez, Joan 624; Bradstreet, Anne 568; Brontë sisters 582; Brooks, Romaine 613; Brownmiller, Susan 632; Curie, Marie 496; Dicks, Dorothea 510; Earhart, Amelia 474; Friedan, Betty 555; Gimke, Angeline 473; Ginke, Sarah 473; Goldman, Emma 521; Hutchinson, Anne 644; Kumin, Maxine 531; Mead, Margaret 553; Millay, Edna St. Vincent 496; Near, Holly 546; Nin, Anais 472; Paley, Grace 531; Raitt, Bonnie 490; Sexton, Anne 476; Stanton, Elizabeth Cady 518; Stuart, Elinore Pruitt 566; Sullivan, Annie 496; Terry, Ellen 589; Van Horne, Harriet 686; Vernon, Mabel 570; Walker, Alice 470, 531; Walker, Mary Richardson 574; Willard, Frances 533; Woolf, Virginia 614, 697; Wright, Frances 534

BIRTH CONTROL/ABORTION
  16mm Films 22, 79, 81
  Videotapes 201, 202, 213, 238
  Slides 429
  Recordings/Spoken 467, 583

BISEXUALITY
  16mm Films 154
  Videotapes 239
  Recordings/Spoken 641

CARTOONISTS, HUMOR
  Videotapes 219
  Recordings/Spoken Tomlin, Lily 635

CHILDBIRTH see MOTHERHOOD...

CHOREOGRAPHY see DANCE...

CRAFTS, CRAFTSPERSONS
  16mm Films 135

DANCE, CHOREOGRAPHERS, DANCERS
  16mm Films Sokolow, Anna 153
  Videotapes 346, 348

DIVORCE see FAMILY...

DRAMA, PLAYWRIGHTS, ACTRESSES
  16mm Films Hansberry, Lorraine 105
  Videotapes 244, 267, 303, 313, 321, 346; Moreau, Jeanne 230
  Filmstrips 408
  Recordings/Spoken 643; Hansberry, Lorraine 543, 544; Lindfors, Viveca 551; Terry, Ellen 589

EDUCATION
    16mm Films 51, 147
    Videotapes 338, 367

EMPLOYMENT, CAREERS (general; see also WORKING MOTHERS)
    16mm Films 28, 42, 104, 126, 128, 133, 141, 183, 186, 187
    Videotapes 208, 219, 250, 255, 261, 274, 301, 323, 328, 333, 344, 346, 349, 353, 362, 369
    Filmstrips 381, 390, 401, 404, 409
    Slides 438
    Recordings/Spoken 594, 617, 636, 648, 668, 686, 714

EQUAL RIGHTS AMENDMENT see LAW, LEGISLATION-- Equal Rights Amendment

FAMILY/MARRIAGE/DIVORCE
    16mm Films 4, 6, 14, 66, 125, 150, 156
    Videotapes 209, 210, 223, 224, 225, 234, 247, 272, 284, 286, 316, 340, 355
    Slides 454
    Recordings/Spoken 587, 602, 603, 619, 625, 645

FEMINIST MOVEMENT--Contemporary
    16mm Films 7, 60, 117, 132, 134, 146, 148, 191
    Videotapes 221, 228, 259, 262, 266, 275, 276, 286, 287, 331, 357, 358, 366, 367
    Filmstrips 373, 399, 400, 401, 402, 410
    Slides 439, 453, 465,
    Recordings/Spoken 493, 499, 548, 554, 555, 562, 567, 690, 691, 692, 696

FEMINIST MOVEMENT--Historical
    16mm Films 7, 82, 148, 161, 169
    Videotapes 240, 271, 290, 319, 368
    Filmstrips 376, 399, 402, 405, 413
    Slides 447
    Recordings/Spoken 492, 493, 502, 511, 512, 518, 533, 570, 591, 622, 696

FILM, FILMMAKERS
    16mm Films 11, 20, 56, 93, 172
    Videotapes 332; Moreau, Jeanne 230; Velasquez, Elaine 352
    Recordings/Spoken 627; Rosen, Marjorie 501

HEALTH (see also ALCOHOLISM)
    16mm Films 29, 75
    Videotapes 215, 216, 296, 314, 315, 343, 363
    Recordings/Spoken 503, 577, 646

HISTORY--Black Women in America
    Recordings/Spoken 485, 486, 487, 488, 489, 581

HISTORY--Women in American History
    16mm Films 43, 45, 51, 52, 53, 64, 71, 77, 118
    Videotapes 240
    Filmstrips 377, 393, 395, 399, 402, 405, 407
    Slides 440
    Recordings/Spoken 473, 475, 566, 574, 592, 609, 644, 680, 698

HISTORY--Women in History
    16mm Films 8, 57, 163, 176, 178
    Videotapes 298, 361
    Filmstrips 371, 373, 378, 380, 406
    Slides 446, 449, 466
    Recordings/Spoken 477, 575, 623, 654, 656, 657, 679, 682, 683, 689

INTERNATIONAL WOMEN
    16mm Films Bolivia 144; Canada 161; Cuba 24; Ireland 129; Korea 58; Latin America 50, 116, 144; Oman 80; Sweden 177; Toubou 190; Vietnam 41, 188; Wales 189
    Videotapes Ireland 294, 295, 356
    Filmstrips France 378
    Slides Canada 446, 449; China 464
    Recordings/Spoken Bangladesh 659; Chile 660; China 661, 693; France 665; India 666; Israel 554; Latin America 667; Peru 471; Sicily 678

INTERPERSONAL RELATIONS (see also SOCIAL ROLES...; SOCIALIZATION)
    16mm Films 72, 94, 110, 124, 127, 138
    Videotapes 365
    Recordings/Spoken 535, 645

LAW, LEGISLATION (see also next entry)
    Videotapes 220, 268, 269, 284, 297, 316, 339, 345
    Recordings/Spoken 564, 650

LAW, LEGISLATION--Equal Rights Amendment
    16mm Films 40, 55
    Videotapes 203, 342, 347
    Recordings/Spoken 522

LESBIANISM
    16mm Films 36, 37, 76, 85, 89, 120, 180, 185
    Videotapes 235, 242, 270, 278, 291, 327
    Recordings/Spoken 565, 641

LITERATURE, AUTHORS
    16mm Films Flanner, Janet 196; Jackson, Shirley 46;

Subject Index

  Morrison, Toni 196; O'Connor, Flannery 32, 47; Welty, Eudora 196
  Videotapes 256, 273, 346, 348; Atwood, Margaret 280; Beauvoir, Simone de 233; Blais, Marie-Claire 282
  Filmstrips 396, 411; Brontë, Emily 375; Cather, Willa 398, 412
  Recordings/Spoken 488, 559, 578, 599, 618, 652, 653, 662, 663, 664, 670, 671, 672, 673, 674, 675, 676, 677, 684, 685; Austen, Jane 478, 479, 480, 481, 482, 483, 590; Auston, Mary 709; Bradstreet, Anne 568; Brontë, Charlotte 491; Brownmiller, Susan 631, 632; Chopin, Kate 484, 707; Colette 498; Eliot, George 514, 515, 516; Gaskell, Elizabeth 537; Glasgow, Ellen 701; Hellman, Lillian 708; Jackson, Shirley 556, 557; Jewett, Sarah 711; Lessing, Doris 509, 700; Nin, Anais 472; Oates, Joyce Carol 706; O'Connor, Flannery 584, 703, 704; Paley, Grace 531; Porter, Katherine Anne 601; Sand, George 539; Stein, Gertrude 540, 705; Stowe, Harriet Beecher 630; Walker, Alice 531; Welty, Eudora 639, 702; Wharton, Edith 640; Woolf, Virginia 614

MARRIAGE see FAMILY...

MENOPAUSE
  Slides 444

MENSTRUATION
  16mm Films 103, 114, 131
  Recordings/Spoken 576

MENTAL HEALTH, ILLNESS
  Videotapes 329
  Recordings/Spoken 504, 586, 649

MINORITIES
  16mm Films 107
  Videotapes 226, 272, 279, 303, 360
  Recordings/Spoken 485, 486, 487, 488, 489, 651, 690

MOTHERHOOD, CHILDBIRTH
  16mm Films 48, 62, 70, 97, 108, 150, 151, 152
  Videotapes 214, 248, 252, 254, 300, 340
  Slides 455
  Recordings/Spoken 529, 577, 692

MUSIC, MUSICIANS
  16mm Films Jackson, Mahalia 109; Reynolds, Malvina 106
  Videotapes 348, 350; Brown, Eileen 243; Ferron 245; Gorton, Ruthie 312; Jessye, Eva 237; Kaplowitz, Betty 212
  Recordings/Spoken 647; Adam, Margie 572; Baez, Joan 624; Near, Holly 546, 558; Raitt, Bonnie 490; Sisters by Choice 626; Sweet Honey in the Rock 633

Subject Index

PHOTOGRAPHY, PHOTOGRAPHERS
  16mm Films Cunningham, Imogen 87, 88
  Videotapes Jacobi, Lotte 231

PHYSICAL FITNESS (see also HEALTH; SELF DEFENSE; SPORTS)
  16mm Films 170

POETRY, POETS
  16mm Films Ruckeyser, Muriel 153, 196
  Videotapes Lawrence, Monica Holden 278; Lord, Audre 229; Piercy, Marge 229; Richards, Beah 258; Shange, Ntozake 246
  Recordings/Spoken 615; Bahat, Amirh 526; Bogan Louise 596; Brown, Lee 563; Browning, Elizabeth Barrett 517; Clark, China 526; Dickinson, Emily 519, 520, 595; Fabio, Sarah Webster 524, 525; Gahn, Judy 588; Giovanni, Nikki 541; Hacker, Marilyn 542, 573; Jong, Erica 560; Kumin, Maxine 531; Larkin, Joan 610; Levertov, Denise 699; Lord, Audre 569, 610; McKnight, Jo Ann 526; Moore, Honor 610; Moore, Marianne 597; Morgan, Robin 579; Parker, Pat 588; Piercy, Marge 571; Pisan, Christine de 497; Plath, Sylvia 593, 598, 712; Porche, Veranda 600; Rich, Adrienne 610; Sanchez, Sonia 616; Sexton, Anne 476, 621; Swenson, May 634; Wakoski, Diane 505, 506; Walker, Alice 470; Wheatley, Phillis 710

POLITICS
  16mm Films 25, 31, 175
  Videotapes 227, 269, 277, 366

PORNOGRAPHY
  Recordings/Spoken 530

POVERTY see WELFARE...

PRISONERS
  16mm Films 18, 102, 157, 168
  Recordings/Spoken 527, 637

PROSTITUTION
  16mm Films 3, 30, 78, 178
  Recordings/Spoken 508, 605, 606

RAPE
  16mm Films 61, 121, 122, 136, 182
  Videotapes 299, 305, 306, 307, 308
  Recordings/Spoken 631

RELIGION, THE CHURCH
  16mm Films 2, 44, 59, 111

Videotapes 221
Recordings/Spoken 638, 683

SELF DEFENSE
16mm Films 5
Videotapes 263

SEX DISCRIMINATION
16mm Films 21, 26, 96, 112
Videotapes 208, 236, 253, 259, 285, 317, 336, 349
Filmstrips 394
Slides 438, 443, 452, 456
Recordings/Spoken 532, 545, 578, 594, 617, 620, 669

SEX ROLES AND STEREOTYPES (see also next two entries)
16mm Films 57, 67, 73, 74, 83, 115, 145, 155, 156, 164, 165, 167, 179, 197
Videotapes 283, 304, 324, 332, 336, 364
Filmstrips 374, 381, 382, 383, 384, 385, 386, 387, 389, 397, 406
Slides 441
Recordings/Spoken 599, 607, 612, 620, 689

SEX ROLES AND STEREOTYPES--In Advertising
16mm Films 17, 96
Videotapes 309
Slides 430, 434
Recordings/Spoken 604, 655

SEX ROLES AND STEREOTYPES--In Schools and Education
16mm Films 12, 28, 100, 147, 184
Videotapes 304, 338
Filmstrips 394
Slides 431, 437, 451

SEXUALITY (see also BISEXUALITY; LESBIANISM)
16mm Films 2, 69, 81
Videotapes 293, 302
Recordings/Spoken 507, 528, 549, 694

SOCIAL ROLES AND VALUES
16mm Films 1, 6, 23, 27, 34, 49, 66, 83, 84, 86, 90, 91, 119, 141, 162, 167, 178
Videotapes 334, 337
Filmstrips 372, 374, 376, 386, 388, 389, 391, 392, 400, 401, 403
Slides 440, 448
Recordings/Spoken 477, 494, 495, 547, 561, 587, 608, 612, 628, 654, 683, 687, 688, 695

SOCIALIZATION
16mm Films 10, 13, 17, 19, 92, 143, 165
Videotapes 236, 241, 336

Filmstrips 385
Recordings/Spoken 468, 550, 586, 612, 628, 636

SPORTS (see also PHYSICAL FITNESS; SELF DEFENSE)
16mm Films 26, 38, 54, 63, 68, 95, 123, 139, 149, 192, 193, 198, 199
Videotapes 292, 326
Recordings/Spoken 580

UNIONIZATION
16mm Films 39, 158, 173
Videotapes 260, 265
Recordings/Spoken 617

VIOLENCE (see also BATTERED WOMEN; RAPE)
Recordings/Spoken 642

WELFARE, POVERTY
16mm Films 174, 195
Videotapes 318
Recordings/Spoken 629

WORKING MOTHERS (see also EMPLOYMENT...)
16mm Films 160, 194, 195
Videotapes 288, 289